# Data Modeling
## Round Trip Engineering
### Using Oracle Data Modeler

A Step by Step Tutorial

Copyright © by Djoni Darmawikarta

# Table of Contents

# Introduction

*Data Modeling Round Trip Engineering Using Oracle Data Modeler* is a step by step data modeling tutorial for beginners.

## ER Data Modeling

The data model you will learn in this book is ER (Entity Relationship) data model.

- An ER data model is made up of entities and their relationships.
- An entity is something about the business that the application/system needs to keep its data (data about the entity).
- An entity has attributes, which define the detail of the entity in terms of data items.

## The Data Modeler

Data Modeler used in this book is a data modeling tool (software) from Oracle.

- The free of charge GUI tool is rich on ER data modeling features.
- We will go through the modeling steps supported by the tool.
- Techniques, such as the "normalization", not supported by the tool, will not be covered.

## The Round Trip

We will step through a round trip, which has two parts: forward engineering and reverse engineering.

- In the forward engineering part (Part I of the book), we will start building a new logical model, forward engineering it to relational and physical models, and completing this part of our trip when we generate the DDL script (Data Definition Language) and run the script to create the database.
- In the reverse engineering part (Part II of the book), we modify the database, import its data dictionary into a relational model, and reverse-engineering the relational to a logical model. Our logical model would then be in synch with the database.

## Prerequisite

Though for beginners of data modeling, this is a technical book.

- You should have relational database working skill.
- My other book, *Oracle SQL*, is a good base to equip you with the skill.

## Book Examples

To learn the most out of this book, try the book examples.

To completely follow the examples, you need to have three pieces of software:

- Data Modeler, the modeling tool. The book uses the Windows version of the tool. Versions for Linux and Mac OSX platform are also available.
- SQL Developer, the GUI IDE (Graphical User Interface Integrated Development Environment) we use to run the DDL script and inspect the resulting database objects.
- Oracle database Express Edition, the RDBMS where we have the database we use during the forward and reverse engineering.

If you have them on your own computer, you can freely and safely follow the examples.

- You can download all of them free of charge from the Oracle website.
- Appendix A guides you to get and set them up.

The book examples are tested on the Windows version of Data Modeler version 4.1.2.895.

- Version 4.1.2.895 was the latest version available from Oracle website at the time of writing this book.
- If you already have a Data Modeler, you can check its version as follows: **Help** > **About**.

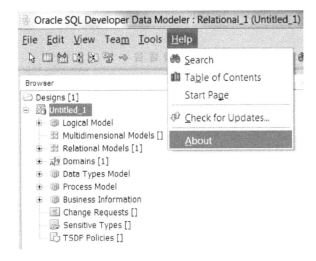

You will see the version on the **About** tab.

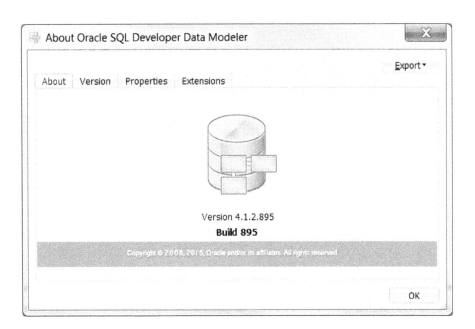

[5]

## Part I: Forward Engineering

Forward engineering moves a logical model to the generation of the database.

■ We will create a data model from scratch.
■ From the new logical model we will go through all the steps to generation of the DDL script (Data Definition Language)
■ We will then run the DDL to create the Oracle database.

Our forward-engineering has the following eight steps:

■ Create logical model
■ Engineer logical to relational model
■ Adding relational object
■ Abbreviating names
■ Creating physical model
■ Adding physical object
■ Generating DDL
■ Creating database

Before we start creating a logical model, we need to understand how Oracle Modeler structure and store its model objects. You will learn these in the first chapter.

# Chapter 1: Design

When you start Data Modeler, as seen on the Browser, a Designs [1] *folder* is opened.

- The name of the folder (Designs) is unchangeable.
- The [1] on the folder indicates it contains 1 (one) *design*, which currently is named Untitled_1. You will see a bit later it has more than 1, when we additional design.

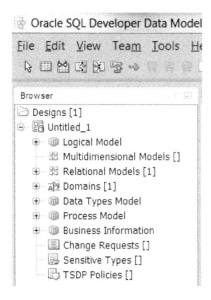

A logical and a relational *diagram* are also opened.

- They (their tabs) are named Logical (Untitled_1) and Relational_1 (Untitled_1) respectively.
- The diagrams are empty as the logical and relational models do not have any object yet.

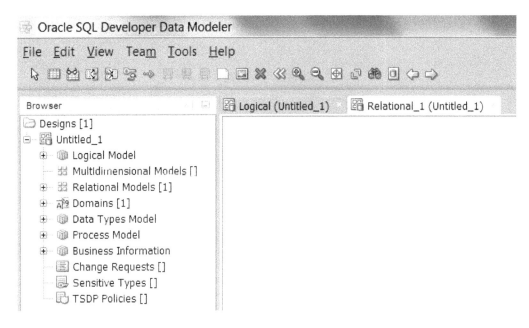

## Renaming Design

You can rename a design by saving it. To rename a design, right click its name and select Save Design.

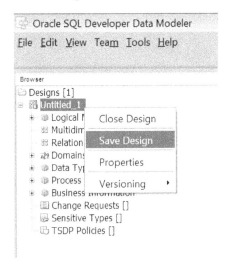

On the Save Design dialog window:

- Enter the name of the design on the File Name field, which in our case we enter Sales.
- Click the Save button to save the design with the name (Sales).

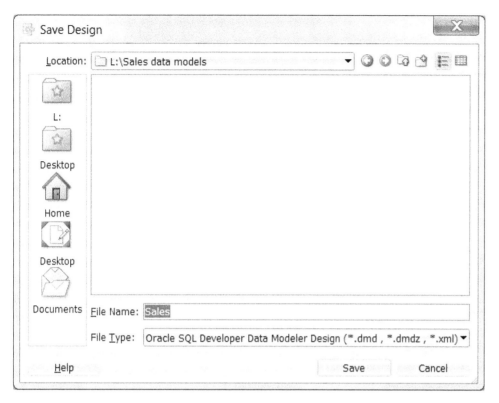

On the folder where you saved the design:

- A Windows sub folder named **Sales** and a file named **Sales**.dmd are created.
- The sub folder contains all the design objects.

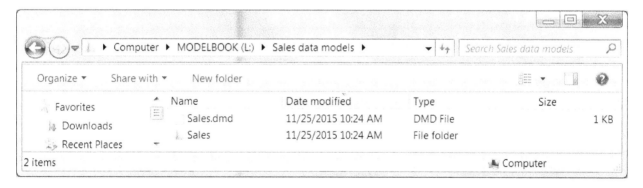

## Sales Design

As a result of saving the design:

- The design name is now Sales.
- The logical and relational diagram tabs are also labeled with Sales (in parentheses).
- We will use the Sales design throughout this book.

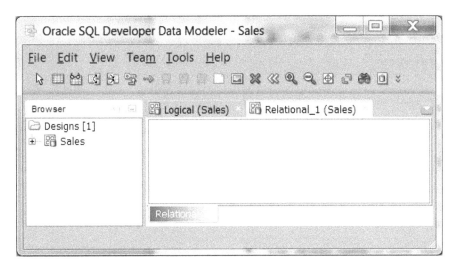

## Saving Design

To avoid major loss of your modeling work, from time to time, you should save your design.

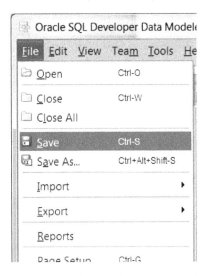

Wait until the saving progress indicator is off before doing anything else.

## Closing Design

You close a design from the File menu and selecting Close. If you have more than one design opened, you can close all of them by selecting Close All.

When you are closing a design you will be prompted:

- Select the model to save, and then click the Save Selected button, or
- Close without Save, or
- Cancel your closing.

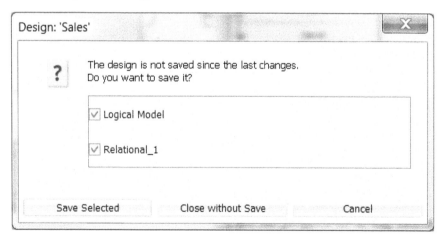

## Deleting Design

If you need to delete a design:

- Delete both the dmd file and the subfolder on the Windows.
- You cannot delete a design from with the Data Modeler; it does not have a facility to delete a design.

## Design Objects

A design, such as our Sales, has ten objects.

- You can see the ten objects by expanding the design node.
- In this book we will work only on the logical and relational models.

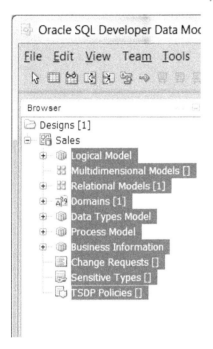

## More Than One Design

A design folder can have more than one design.

To add a design:

- Right click the folder.
- Select New Design.

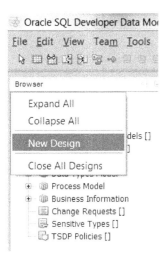

The Design folder has changed:

- The number in the square brackets is now 2 indicating the folder has two designs.
- Untitled_2 design is added.

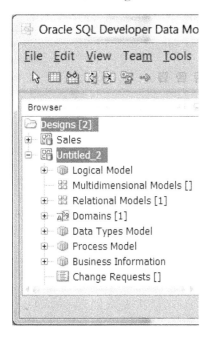

We will work on one design, the Sales design, in this book.

- Remove (delete) the Untitled_2 by closing it.
- We can remove the Untitled_2 design by closing it only because we have not saved it.
- If we already saved it, we would have to delete its Windows folder and file (see the previous Deleting Design section)

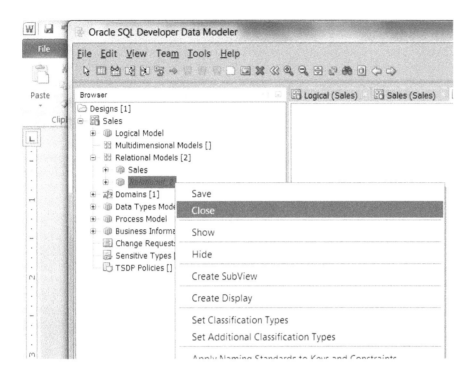

# Chapter 2: Logical Model

A design can only have one logical model named Logical Model.

- You cannot change the name.
- In this book we will use the Sales design we saved earlier.

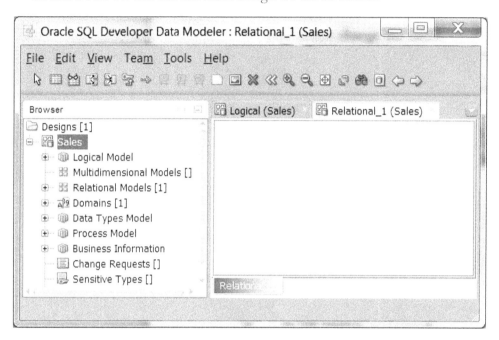

## Logical Model Objects

If you expand the Logical Model node, you will see the logical model objects.

- The six logical objects are: Entity, Relation, Inheritance, View, SubView, and Display.
- In this book we will create all these six objects.

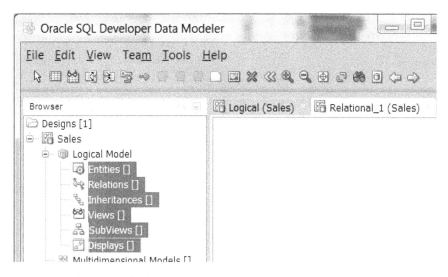

When we finish with this chapter we will have created a logical data model that has its ERD (Entity Relationship Diagram) look like the following.

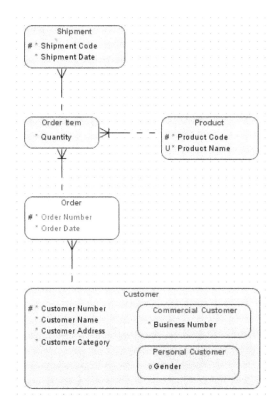

## About entity drawing

■ An entity is drawn as a rounded-corners box.

- The entity name is at the top inside the box with its attributes listed underneath.
- Our logical model has a total of seven entities, two of which are subtype entities.
- The two subtype entities (Commercial Customer and Personal Customer) belong to the Customer entity.

## About relation drawing

- A relation line relates two entities.
- Solid line attached to an entity indicates the entity mandatory; dotted indicates optional. For example, in the Customer to Order relation:
  - The solid line on the Order indicates it must have a Customer.
  - The dotted line on the Customer indicates it can have no Order.
- A line with crow-foot attached to an entity indicates one or more possible occurrence of the entity for one occurrence of the related entity. For example, in the Customer to Order relation, the crow-foot on the Order indicates a customer can have one or more order.
- A cross on the line near an entity indicates that the unique identifier of the related entity becomes the entity's (or part of its) unique identifier. For example, in the Order to Order Item relation, the cross on the line near the Order Item indicates that the Order's identifier (Order Number) is migrated as part of the Order Item's unique identifier; and similarly, the Product Code. The two migrated unique identifiers (Order Number and Product Code) becomes that unique identifier of Order Item.
  - This migrated unique identifier is called **foreign** unique identifier as opposed to the entity's own unique identifier called **primary** unique identifier.

## Attribute Tags

On the drawing, an attribute has a tag on its left. The following table lists the tag and its meaning.

| Tag | Meaning |
| --- | --- |
| #' | Primary unique identifier (must have a value/not null and unique), e.g. Order's Order Number |
| U | Unique identifier (must be unique but can be null), e.g. Product's Product Name |
| * | Mandatory (must have a value/cannot be null), e.g. Order's Order Date |
| o | Optional (can have no value/can be null), e.g. Personal Customer's Gender |

## Diagram Notation

You can choose one of the three diagram notations offered by Data Modeler.

- A notation has its own drawing style of the entities and attributes.

- Our diagram uses the Barker notation, which is my preference (this book uses Barker notation)
- You can choose any one the other two notations (Bachman or Information Engineering) by right-clicking the empty space and select your preferred notation.

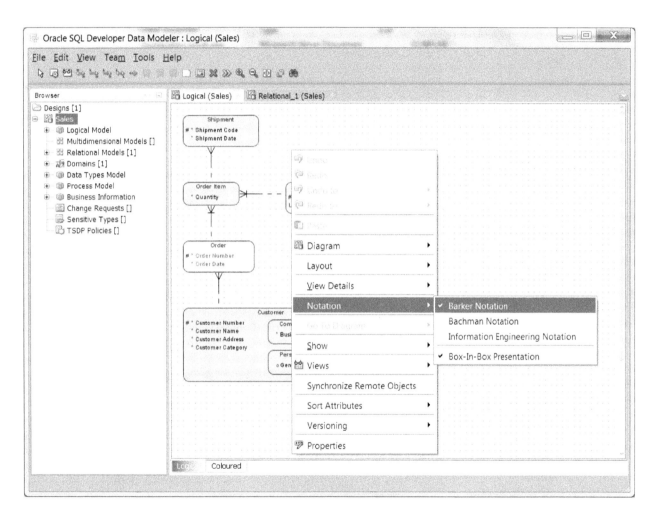

## Entity Object

We will start to create the entities of our Sales design.

If you already closed the design, open it: File > Open.

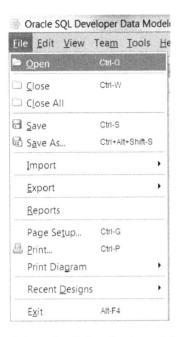

Select the Sales.dmd model file on the folder where you saved it, and then click the Open button.

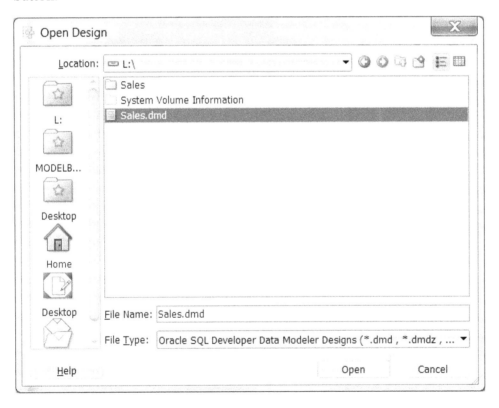

On the "Select Relational Models" window:

- Select the relational model(s) you want to open, including the physical model(s) if you want to
- Click the OK button.

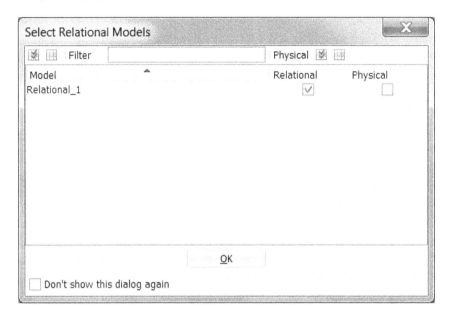

Make sure the Logical tab is open. The diagram is still empty as we have not created any logical object.

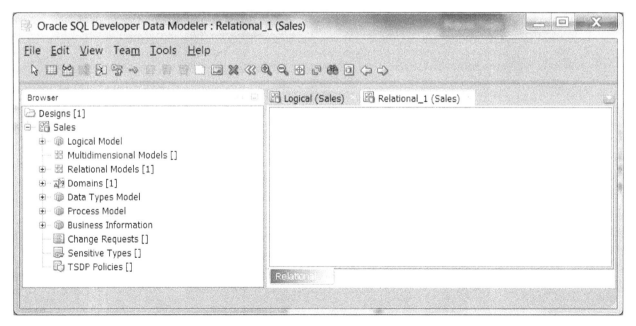

Creating Entity

We will now create the five entities and two subtype entities.

## Order entity

The first entity we will create is the Order entity.

Click the New Entity icon.

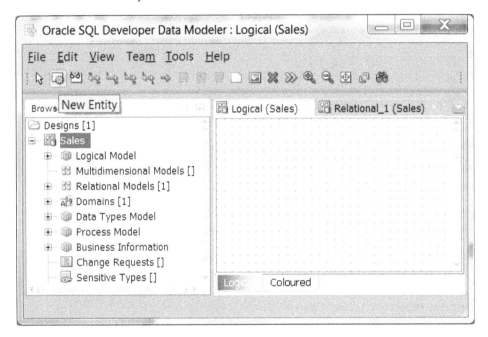

When you now move the cursor into the canvas (where you draw an ER diagram) it will change into a cross + shape.

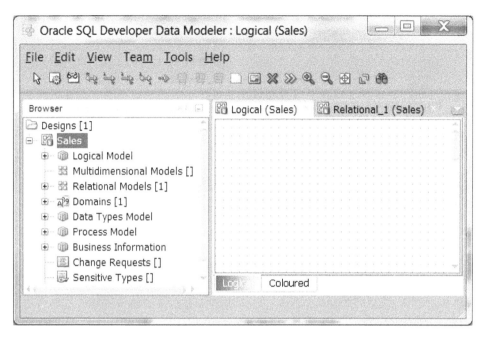

Create a new entity by clicking the + cursor on the canvas. An Entity Properties window will be shown.

**Entity Properties - Entity_1**  ✕

| General | | |
|---|---|---|
| Attributes | | |
| Unique Identifiers | **General** | |
| Relationships | | |
| Subtypes | Name | Entity_1 |
| Volume Properties | Short Name | |
| Engineer To | Synonyms | |
| Comments | Synonym to display | |
| Comments in RDBMS | Preferred Abbreviation | |
| Overlapping Attributes | Long Name | Entity_1 |
| Notes | Based on Structured Type | ▼ |
| Impact Analysis | Super Type | ▼  Select |
| Measurements | Source | |
| Change Requests | Allow Type Substitution: | ☑ |
| Responsible Parties | Create Surrogate Key: | ☐ |
| Documents | Deprecated | ☐ |
| Dynamic Properties | | |
| User Defined Properties | | |
| Classification Types | | |
| Summary | | |

OK    Apply    Naming Rules    Cancel    Help

Change the Name into Order.

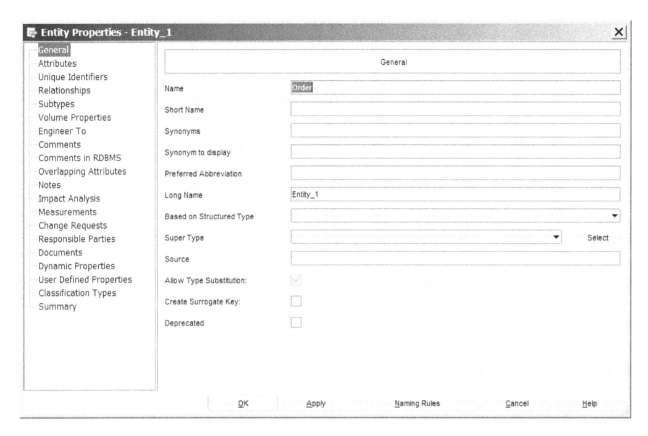

## Order Attributes

We will next add the attributes of the Order entity.

Select Attribute on the left list, and on its right pane, on the Details tab, click the + icon.

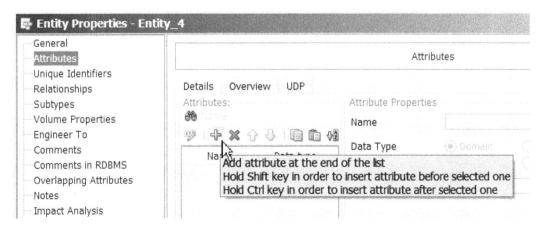

Change the attribute's name into Order Number. Select the **Logical** data type button and VARCHAR **source type** from the drop down list.

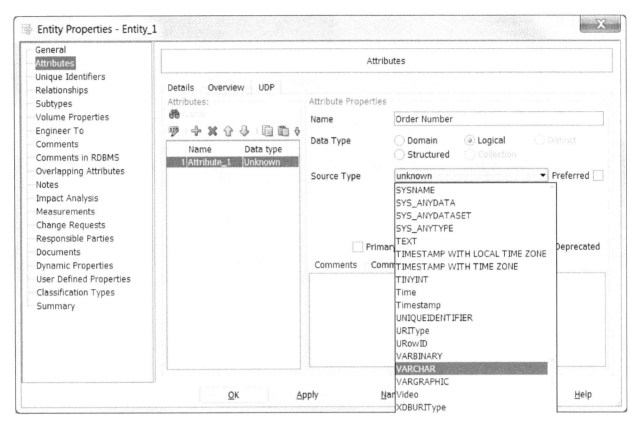

Specify 4 as its size.

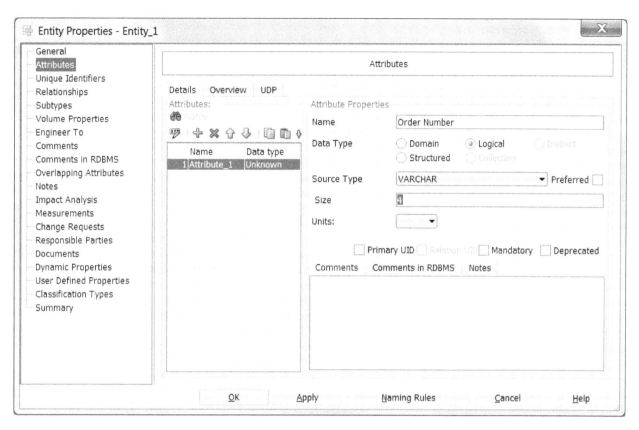

We want the Order Number to be the primary unique identifier of the Order entity, so check the Primary UID box. (UID = Unique Identifier)

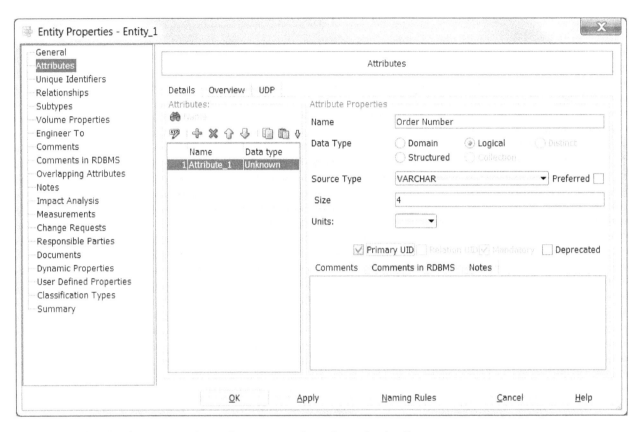

Click the "Apply" button to show the re-named attribute in the list.

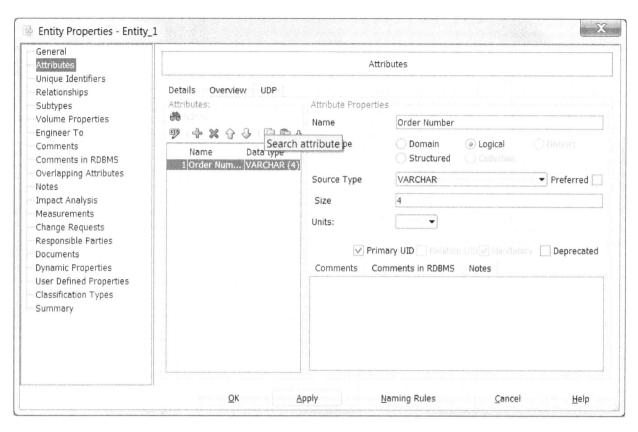

Click the + again to add the next attribute, Order Date, and specify its Date data type.

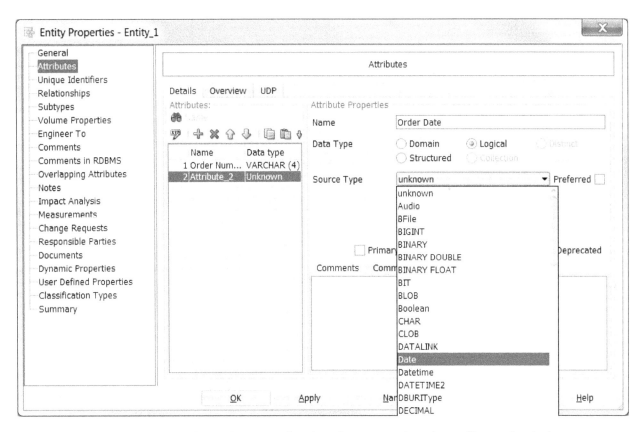

We want the Order Date to always have a value (we don't want it to be null), so check the "Mandatory" box.

We're done with the Order entity, so click the OK button.

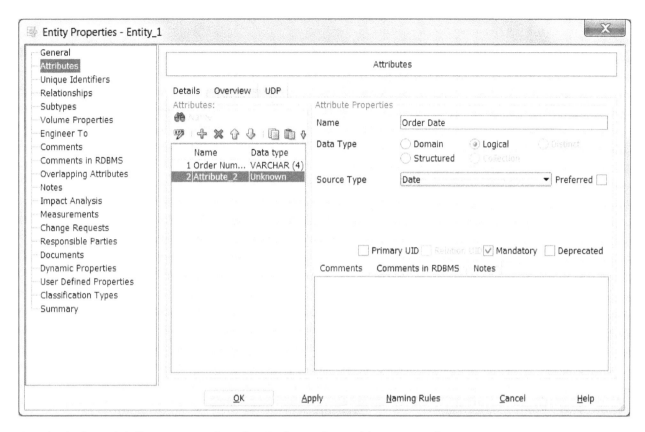

Our logical model diagram now has the Order entity and its two attributes.

- The # label indicates that the attribute is a primary unique identifier; the * indicates that the attribute is mandatory (must have a value, not null).
- Note that a primary unique identifier is always mandatory.

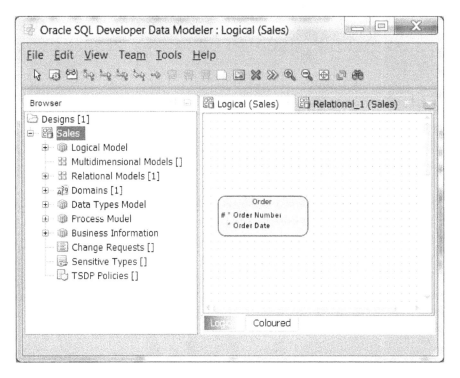

Our cursor is still loaded with the Entity icon. To unload it, click the Select (arrow).

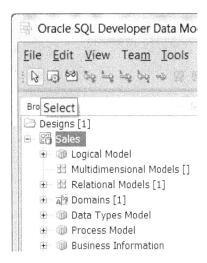

On the Browser you can see the Order entity.

- You might need to expand the Logical Model node by clicking its +

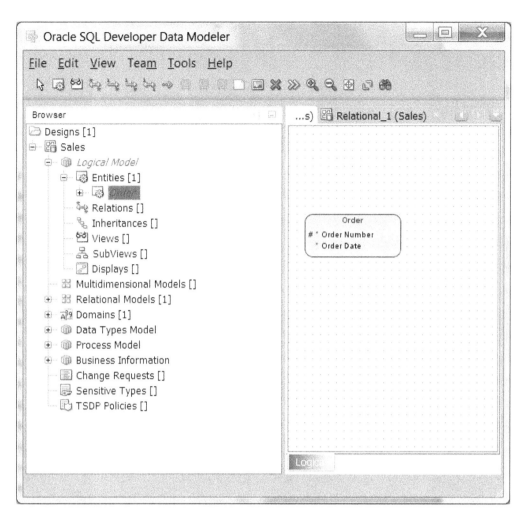

To see its attributes, you need to expand the Order entity by clicking its +

- The two attributes are now visible.
- The [1] on the Entities indicate that the logical model has one entity.

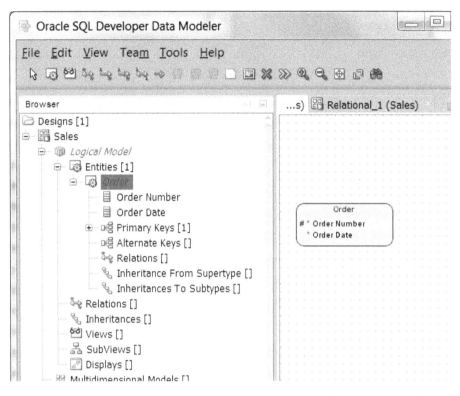

You can similarly expand the Primary Key node see the primary unique identifier's detail.

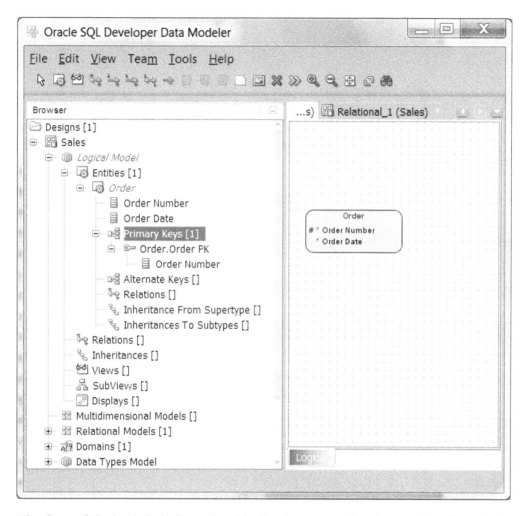

The font of Order is in italic and red indicating something is not right about it; in this case reminding us that we have not saved the change (the new entity)

Save the design and then click the Order entity, it will turn to normal and black.

## Changing the Default of Data Type

By default (out of the box), the Domain radio button is checked.

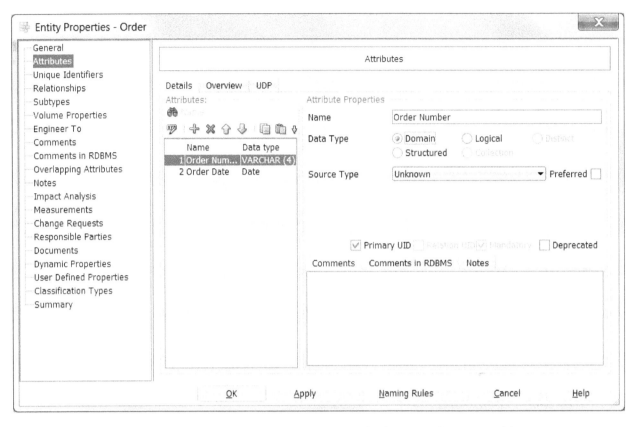

So that you don't need to change from "Domain" to "Logical" every time you add an attribute, go to "Tools" then "Preferences".

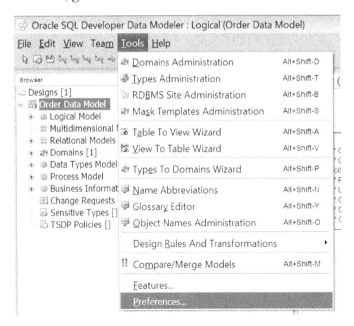

On the "Preferences" window, select "Logical" Datatype, and then click the OK button to close the window.

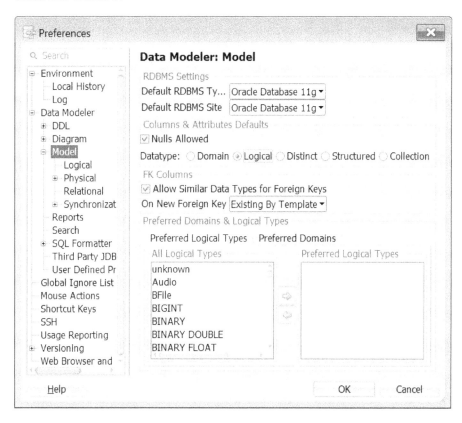

Next, we are adding all the other entities the same steps as we did the Order entity. The following screens respectively show each of the additional entities and their attributes: Customer, Order Item, Product, and Shipment.

## Customer entity

For the Customer Entity:

- Customer Number is the primary key
- All other attributes are mandatory.

## Order Item entity

We create one attribute only: Quantity, which is mandatory.

- The Order entity gets its primary key from its relation with Order and Product entity. (We will add the relations a bit later in this chapter)

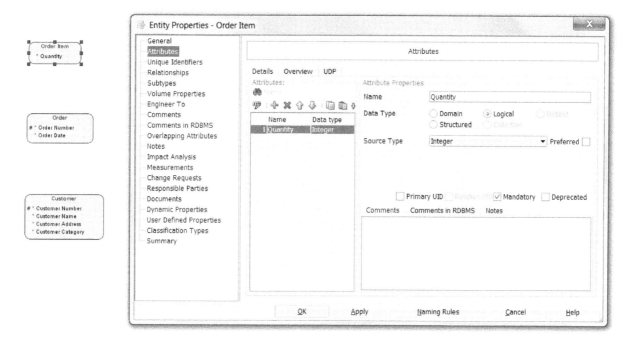

## Product entity

For the Product entity, Product Code is the primary unique identifier.

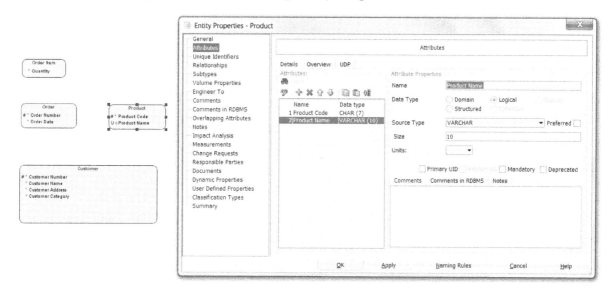

We want the Product Name attribute to be unique (no two product names can be the same). So, select the Unique Identifiers on the left list and click the + to add a unique identifier.

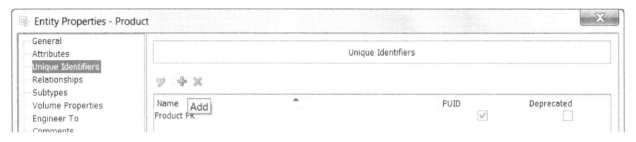

Double-click the new unique identifier Key_1 (default name)

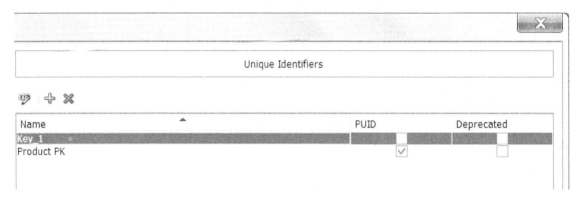

Change the name of the key.

As we want the Product Name to be the unique identifier, on the Attributes and Relations, select the Product Name and click the Add arrow.

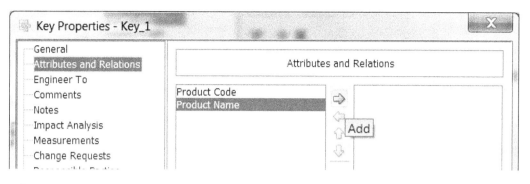

Click OK.

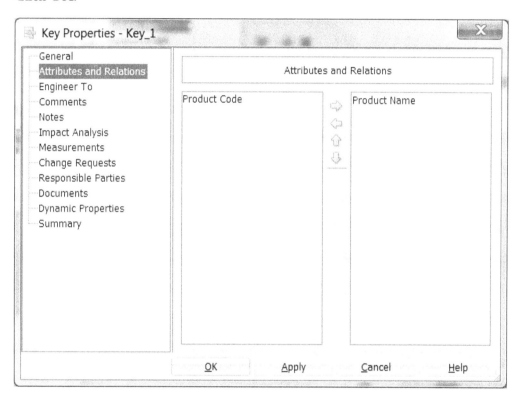

We finish with the Product entity, so click the OK button.

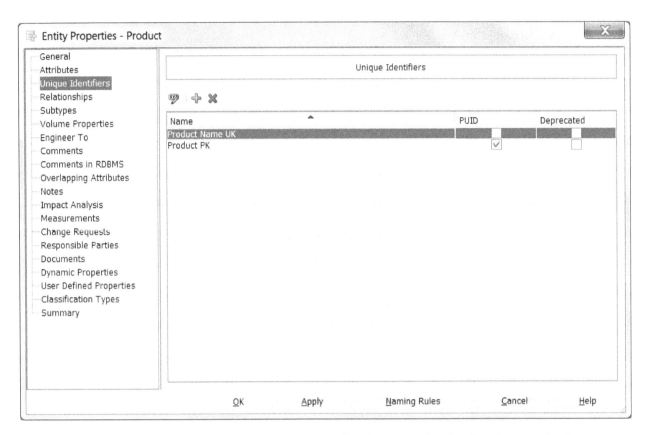

We now have the Product entity on the diagram. Notice the U on the Product Name, that's a label on the attribute specified as unique identifier. The o indicates the attribute is optional (can be null). So, the Product Name can be null, but if it has a value the value must be unique.

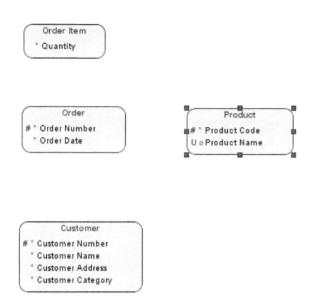

On the Browser, you can see the unique identifier is under the Alternate Keys.

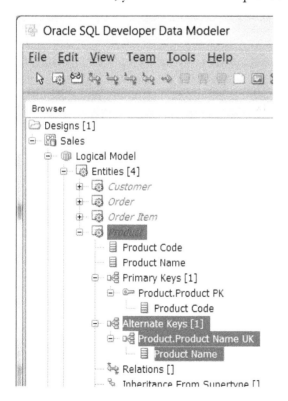

## Shipment entity

For the Shipment entity:

- Shipment Code is the primary key.
- Shipment Date is a mandatory attribute.

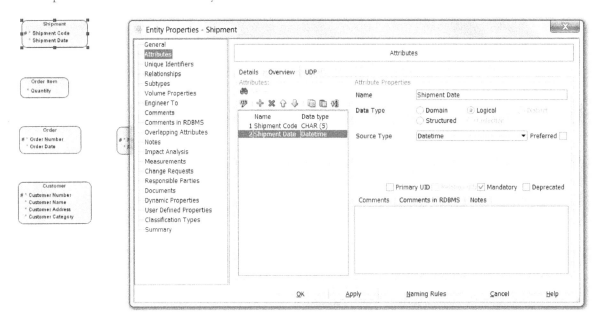

If you look at the Browser, you will see that we now have five entities, indicated by the 5 in the square brackets.

## Attribute Tags

An attribute(s) has a tag on its left.

- The following table lists the tag and its meaning.

- Primary unique identifier has two tags: #*

| Tag | Meaning |
|---|---|
| # | Primary identifier, must have a value/not null and unique |
| U | Unique identifier, must be unique but can have no value/null |
| * | Mandatory (must have a value/cannot be null) |
| O | Optional (can have no value/can be null) |

## Customer Subtype Entities

If you look back at the beginning of this chapter, the Customer entity in our completed logical model has two subtype entities: Commercial Customer and Personal Customer. I'm showing again the completed logical model here for our convenient reference.

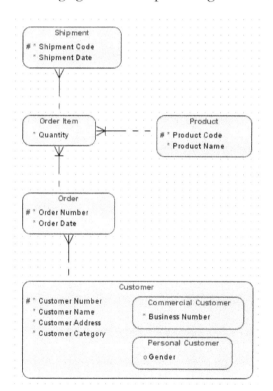

We will now add these two subtype entities. Let's start with the Commercial Customer.

## Commercial Customer

Add an attribute, Business Name, which is mandatory.

To make an entity a subtype of another entity, on the General, select the Super Type entity, which in our case is the Customer entity.

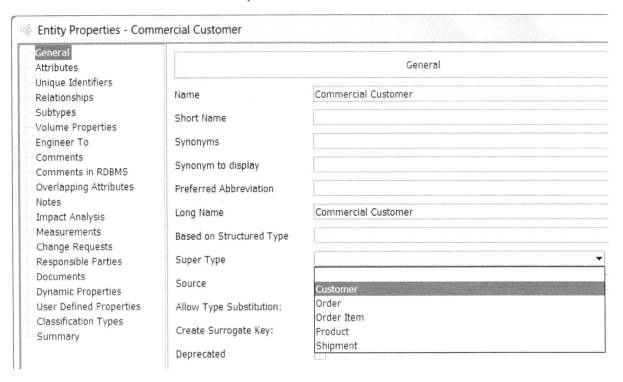

When you then click the OK button, the Commercial Customer entity is within the Customer box. It is a subtype of the Customer entity.

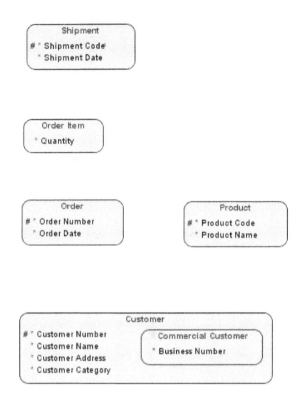

Note: If the Customer/Commercial Customer are not clearly visible, resize the objects by right-clicking on the empty space and select Layout > Resize Objects to Visible.

**Appendix B: Diagramming has more about changing the layout and others on the diagram.**

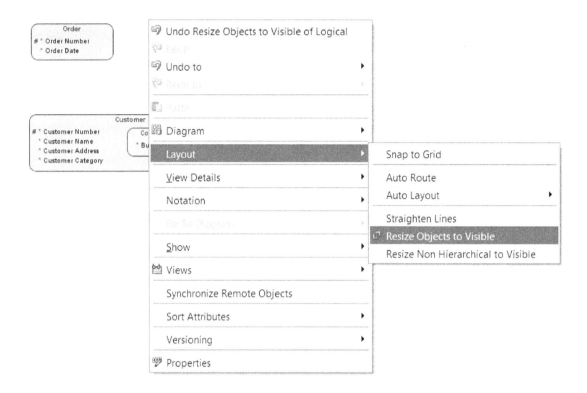

## Personal Customer

Using the same steps, add our 2<sup>nd</sup> entity subtype, the Personal Customer. Note that we'd like the Gender attribute to be optional (not mandatory), that it can be null (has no value).

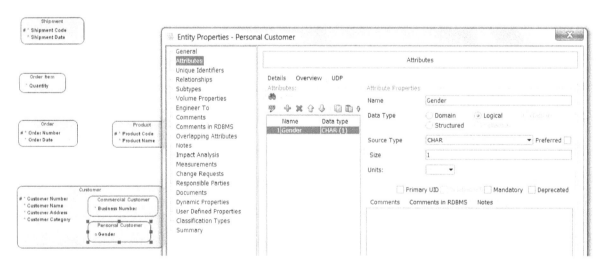

On the Browser, you will now see seven entities in our logical model.

## Inheritance object

An Inheritance shows the relationship between an entity and its subtype. On the Browser you will see that we now have two inheritances. Expand the folder to see them. They show the two customer subtypes of the Customer entity.

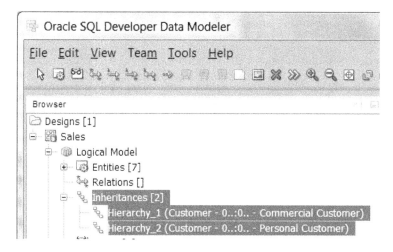

## Relation Object

Having created the entities of our logical model, we will now start to relate them.

- Order to Order Item
- Product to Order Item
- Order Item to Shipment
- Customer to Order

Make sure the Order design and its Logical tab are open.

## Order to Order Item

To start with, we want to relate Order to Order Item.

- Their relation is from Order to Order Item.
- This is one-to-many (1:N), as one order can have more than one item, and
- The Order's primary unique identifier to become the primary unique identifier of the Order Item (identifying).
- To add this relation, click the "New 1:N Relation Identifying" icon.

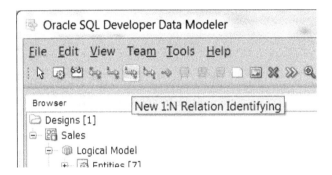

When you then move and the cursor enter the canvas will changes to +/

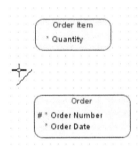

To relate Order to Order Item, click on the Order and release.

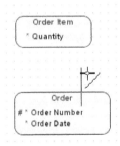

Then move the cursor towards the Order Item and click it inside the entity. The Relation Properties window will be displayed. Click the OK button to close the window.

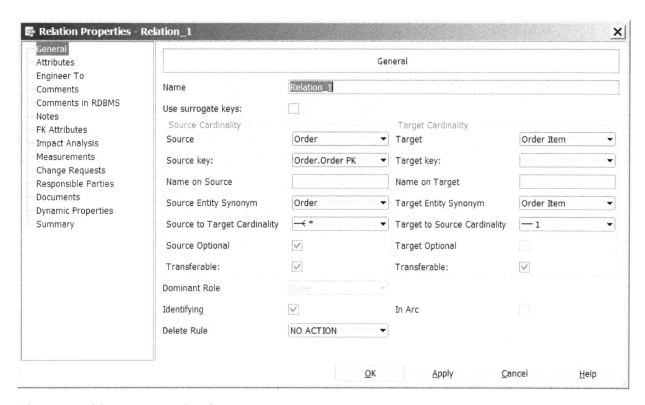

The two entities are now related.

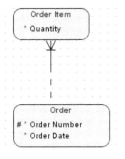

When you double-click the Order Item entity, its properties window will be displayed.

- When you then select its Attributes, you will see an attribute named Order_Order Number that is migrated from the Order's primary unique identifier (Order Number).
- Thanks to the Identifying relation, this primary unique identifier becomes the primary unique identifier of the Order Item.
- If you don't like the name of this attribute (Order_Order Number), you can change it by double-clicking the attribute name.

On the Attribute Properties window, change the name, click the Apply button, and close the window by clicking the OK button.

On the Browser you will see one Relation. Expand the folder to see them. This is the relationship we just added.

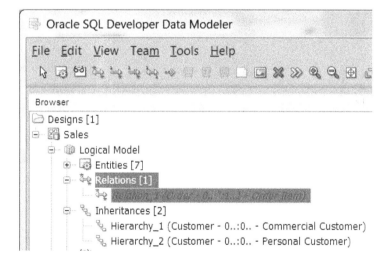

## Product to Order Item

Next, we relate Product to Order item. We add their relationship the same way as we related Order to Order Item. When we're done with this relationship, our (partial) logical diagram now shows the relationship.

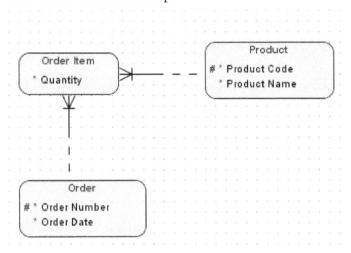

The Order Item's primary unique identifier now consists of two attributes: one from the Order entity; the other from the Product entity.

## Order Item to Shipment

The only difference of the relation from Order to Shipment differs from the previous two relations is that this relation is non-identifying 1:N Relation.

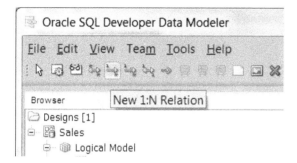

When we're done with this relationship, our (partial) logical diagram now shows the relationship.

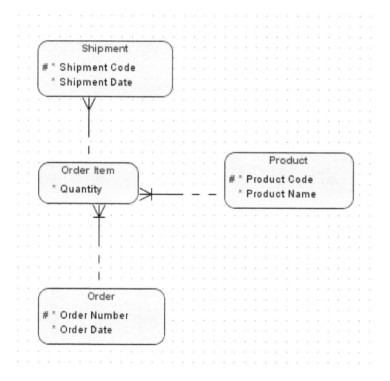

## Customer to Order

This relationship is the same type (non-identifying) as the Order Item to Shipment relationship.

When we're done with this relationship, our logical diagram now shows all relationships we want on the logical model.

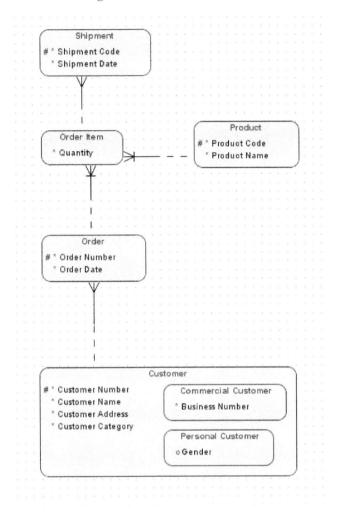

We have now created three of the six logical model objects: Entity, Relationship, and Inheritance.

We will next work on the other three: View, SubView, and Display.

## View Object

A view is a virtual entity.

- Its attributes are from one more entities.
- A view eventually generates into a database view.

To create a view, click the "New View" button and click the loaded cursor on the Logical canvas.

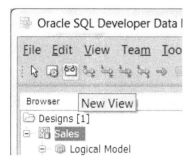

On the View Properties window:

- Change the name, and then click the Query.
- Check the "Auto Join on Relationships" box.

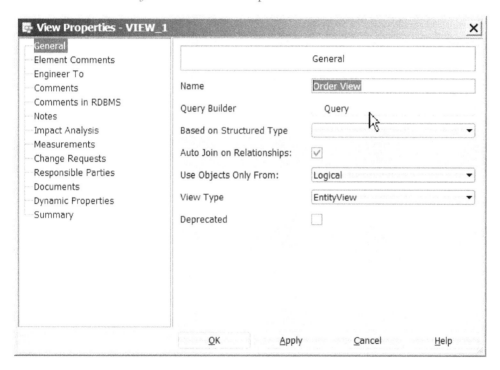

Select the entities you want to be included in the view (e.g. Customer, Order and Order Item) and drag them to the Main tab.

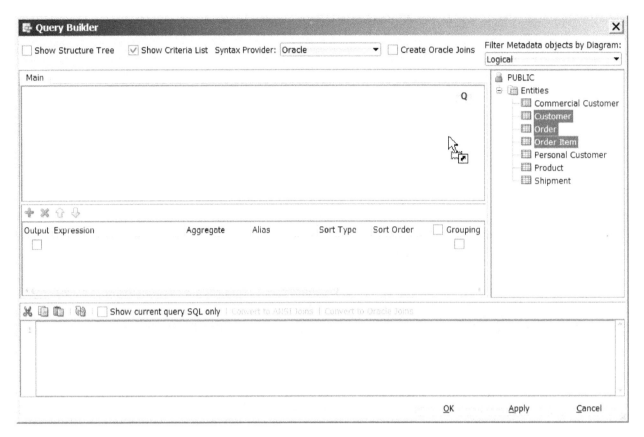

The Query Builder window is now populated with the definition (the specification) of our View.

- The Main panel shows the three entities related.
- The bottom pane shows the SQL. As we have joints in the view and we want to generate the view in Oracle, click the "Convert to Oracle Joins".

If you are familiar with writing SQL query you can update the SQL statement. You can read my other book, *Oracle SQL*, to learn SQL.

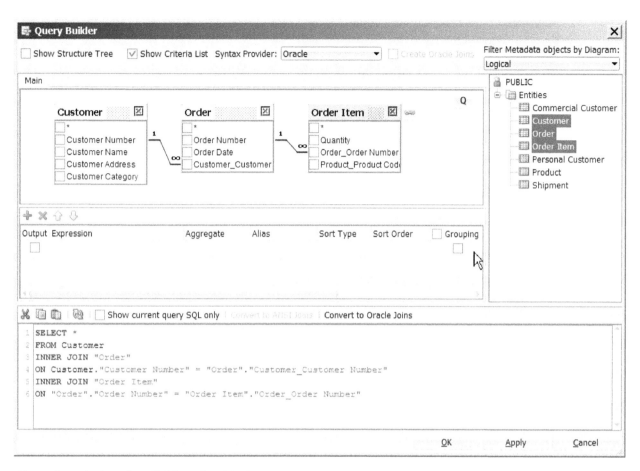

Close the window by clicking the OK button.

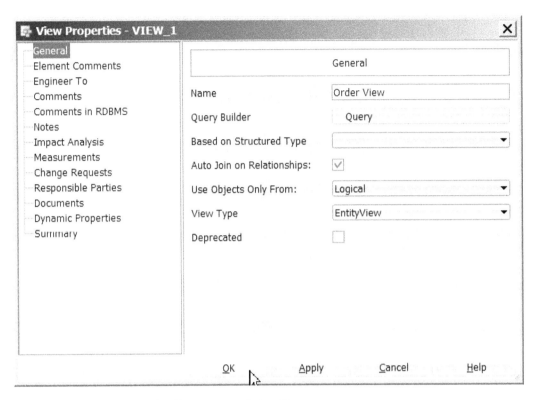

The view is shown on the Browser and the diagram.

- The default colour of the view entity box is different from that of the (regular) entities.
- The box is divided into three parts:
    - The view name as on the top part.
    - The attributes included in the view are listed on the middle part.
    - The entities, from which the view gets the attributes, at the bottom part.

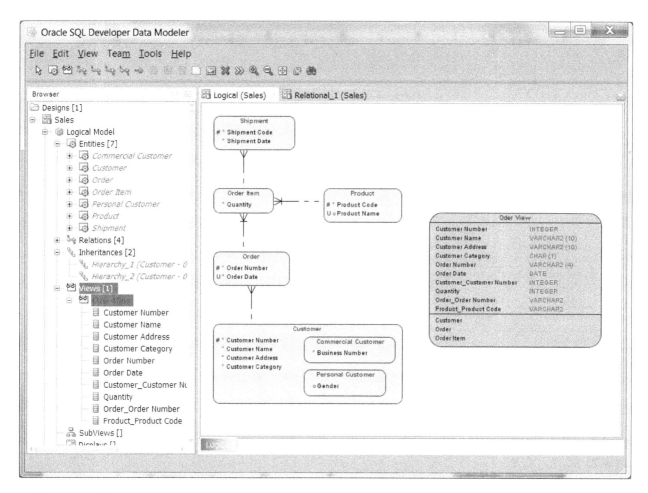

## SubView Object

If your model is complex (has many entities and relations), its ERD can be difficult to visualize. You can create one or more subviews.

A subview:
- Is not a subordinate of a view (database view we covered earlier)
- Is a collection of some of the model's entities of your choice for a specific purpose, to have the selected entities visualized together better than together with the other entities.
- Can also contain, in addition to entities, one or more view.
- Is also known as a **subject area**.

To create a Subview expand the logical model folder, right click the SubView [ ] > New Subview. A subview tab will be opened.

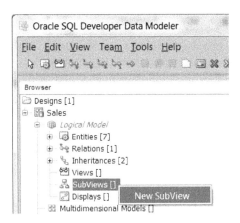

The default name is Logical – SubView_1 (Sales) as seen on the Browser as well on the tab.

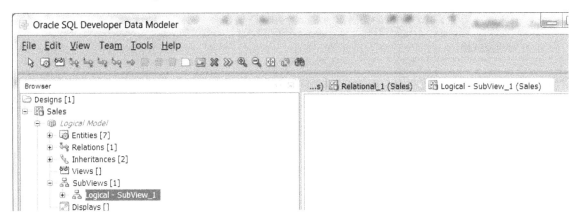

You can change the name of the subview by right clicking on the empty space of the subview diagram and select "Properties".

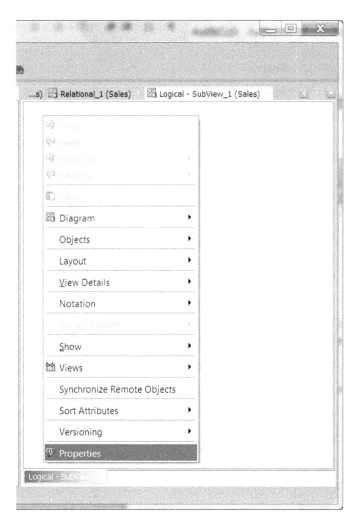

Update the name as you want and then click the OK button.

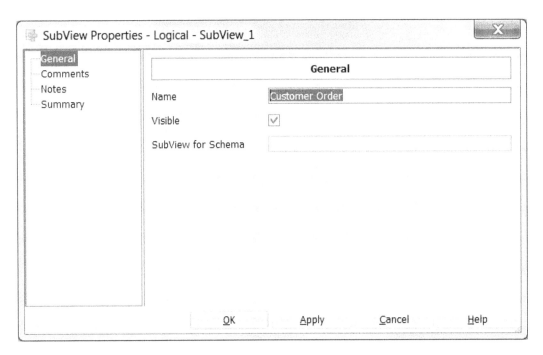

Notice the tab name is now Customer Order (Order). Customer Order is the SubView's name, which is a SubView of the Sales (whole) model.

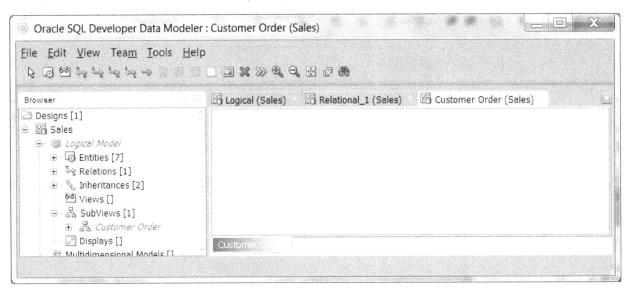

Note that you can create additional subviews from the logical model (one logical model can have multiple subviews).

To add objects (entities and views) into a SubView, right-click on the SubView's tab and select Add/Remove Objects.

On the Entities tab, select the entities (by checking their check boxes) you want to include in the SubView, and then click the Apply button. (The Close button simple close the window, it does not apply your selection)

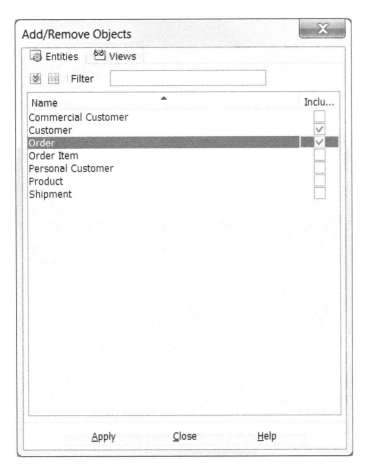

We can also include views in a SubView.

- You can select the views from the list on the View tab.
- We only have one view, the Order View, but we don't want to include any in our SubView, so click the Close button.

You will see the selected entities on the subview diagram.

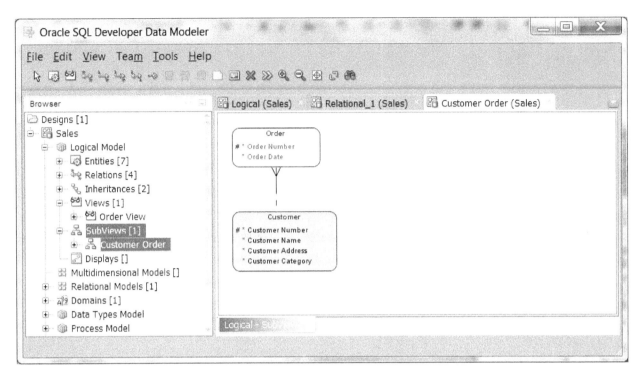

## Display Object

A Display is a version of a diagram. Each display has its own characteristics, e.g. entity background colour, font, and objects displayed.

- Display tab(s) is at the bottom.
- Currently we have the Logical display only as the logical diagram has only this version of its display.

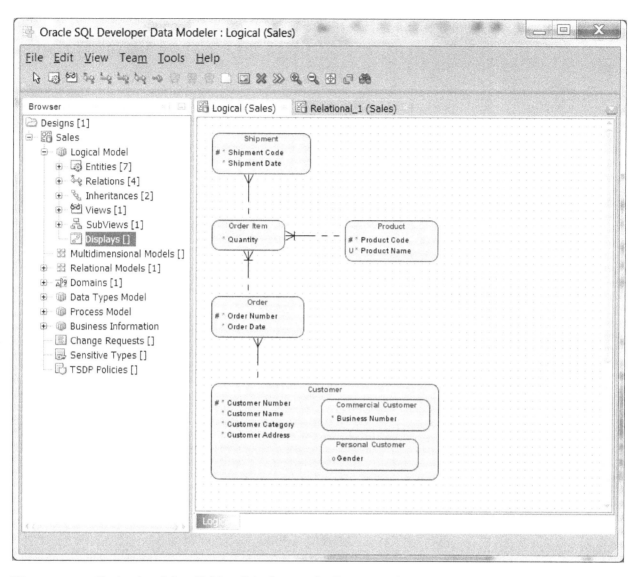

You create a display by right-clicking Display on the Browser, then New Display.

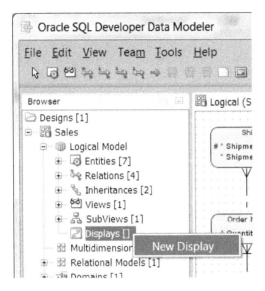

A display named Display_1 (default name) is created.

- A tab named Display_1 is added.
- Display_1 is a clone of the display being selected when you are creating the new display Display_1.

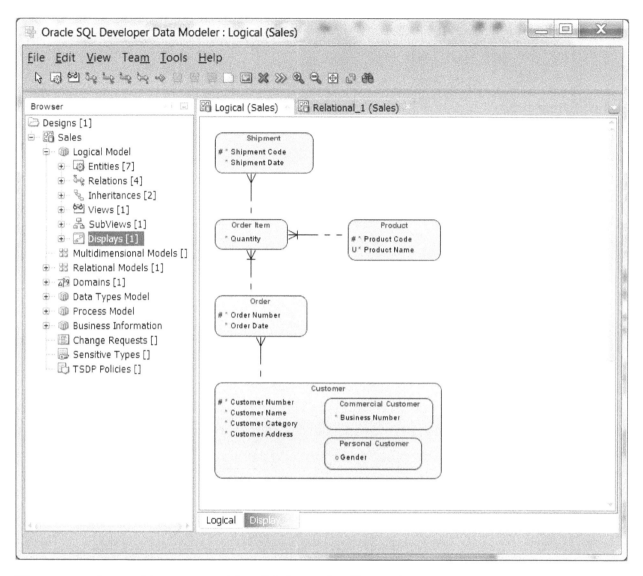

We want to change this name, so right-click it to select Properties.

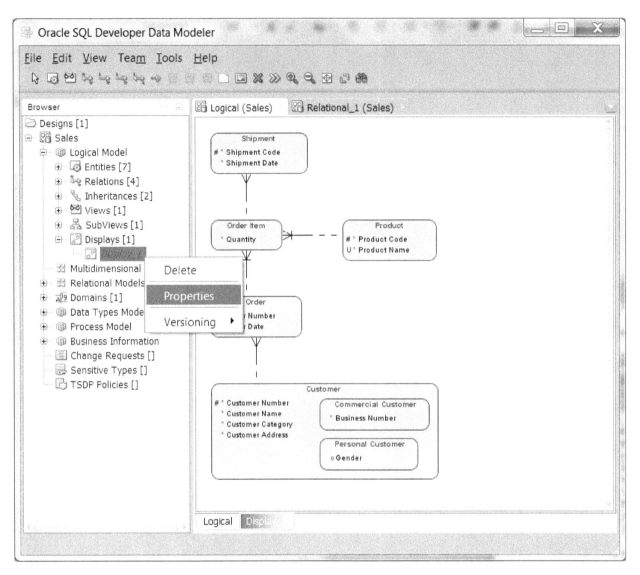

Change the name to Coloured, and then click the OK button.

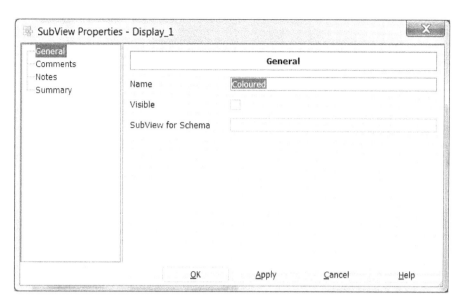

The display has changed.

- Its name is now Coloured, both on the Browser and the tab.
- Everything about Coloured display is copied from Logical display.

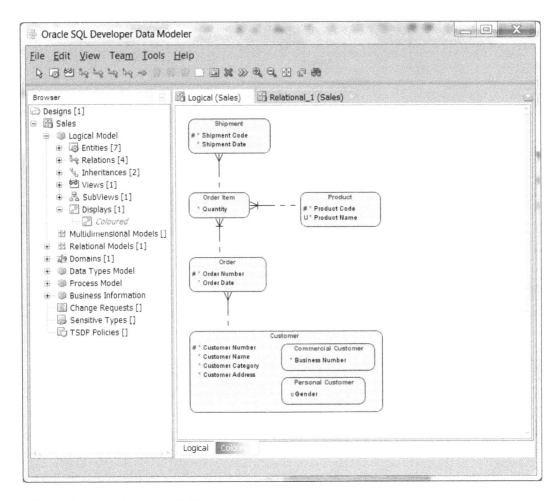

## Changing Colour and Font

Let's now change some colour of the Coloured display.

Right-click the entity you want to customize its colour and select "Format".

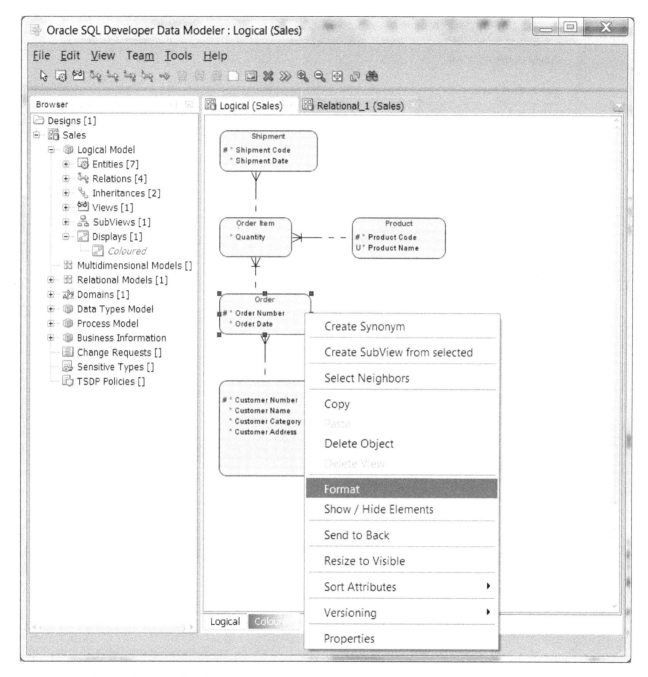

To change the Background or Border color:

- Deselect the "Use Default Format" box.
- If you want the changes applied to only this Display only, check the "Apply to this view only" box; otherwise, all displays will be affected.

To change the background color of the entity, click the colour value (is now light blue). On the "Select Background Color" select the new colour you want and then click the OK button (I selected light green below).

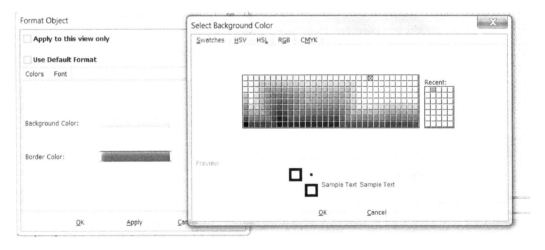

When you next click the "Apply" button, the Order entity's background colour will now be the light green

Similarly you can change the font color on the "Font" tab. Select the item you want change its font colour; e.g. the Attribute.

I'm changing it from black to red.

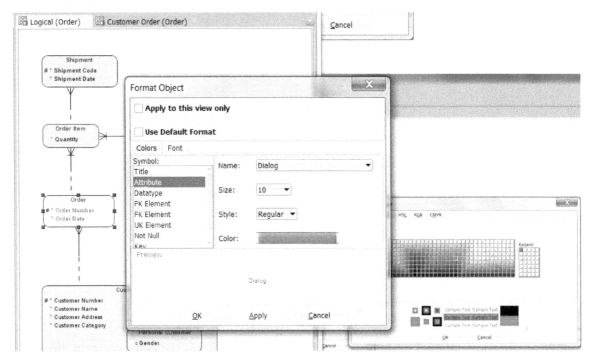

You can create one or more displays. Just follow the steps above to create more displays.

## View Details

You can choose the parts to show on a Display, e.g. entity names only.

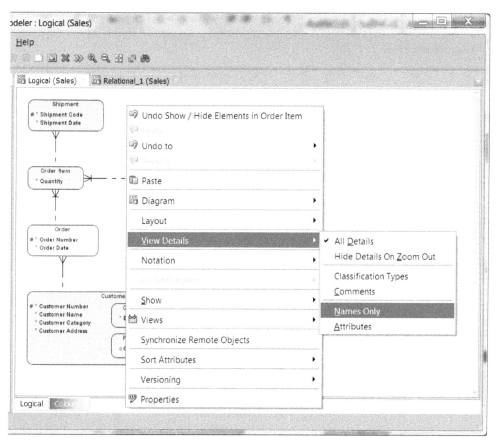

The Display diagram will now look like the following.

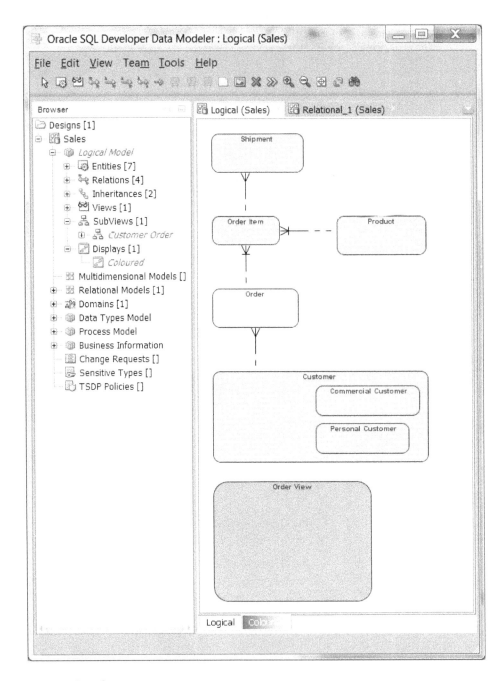

## Show/Hide

When you right-click an entity, Show/Hide Elements is available on the pop-up menu.

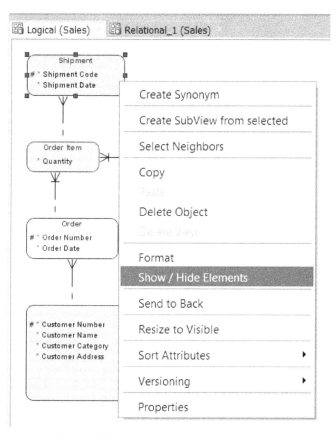

On the Show/Hide Elements window you can select the element to show/hide. I select all to be hidden and this hiding is for this Display (view) only.

Our Coloured display now looks like the following. The Shipment entity shows only its name.

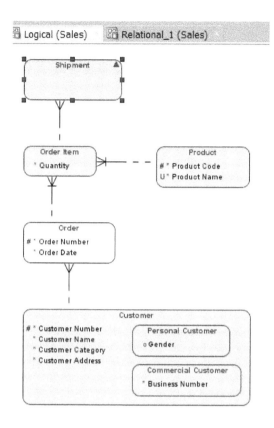

Now that we have the logical model completed, we can engineer it to create its relational model.

# Chapter 3:  Relational Model

When you look at the Browser, you will see the objects of the Relational Model are not exactly the same as those of the Logical Model.

- Only the View, SubView, and Display are the same; the others (the four objects I highlighted) are only on the relational.
- Table is engineered from Entity; Foreign Key from Relation.
- Schema is specific in relational.

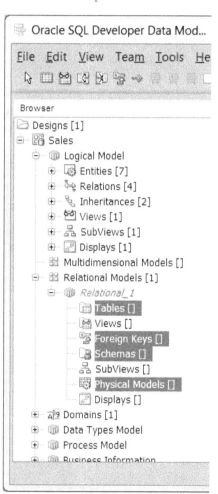

## Relational cf. Logical

While a relational model is for implementation specifically on RDBMS technology (relational database management system); the logical model is independent of any specific technology implementation.

- We can implement a logical model in more than one technology. The only 'constraint' of our logical model is that is an Entity Relationship (ER) model.
- You can for example implement our ER logical model, in addition to relational, as paper filing system. You can implement an entity, or related entities, of your choice, for example in a paper form.

### Engineer to Relational Model

To engineer to a relational model, you need to have an empty relational model (a relational model that does not have any object).

If you don't have, create a new one by right-clicking the Relational Model on the Browser.

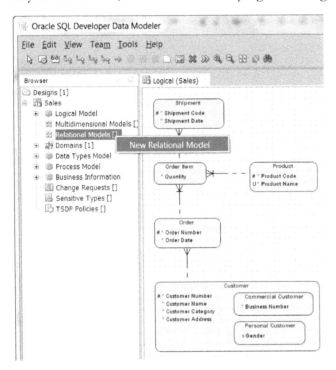

You now have Relational_1.

- To change the name, right-click it, and then select Properties.

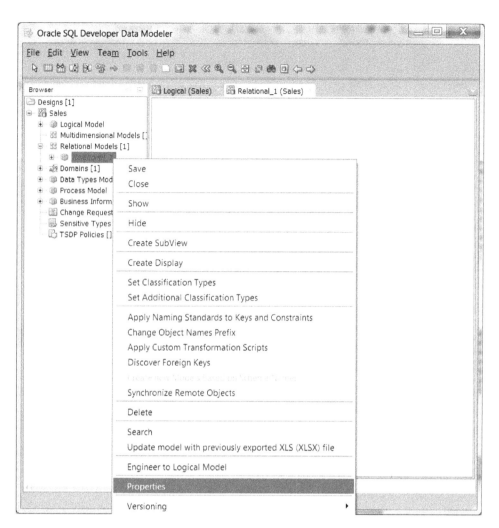

On the Model Properties window, change the name and click the OK button.

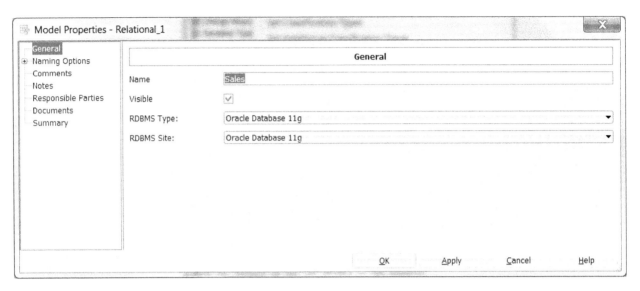

We can now engineer the logical model into this "Sales" relational model.

- Right-click the Logical Model > Engineer to Relational Model.

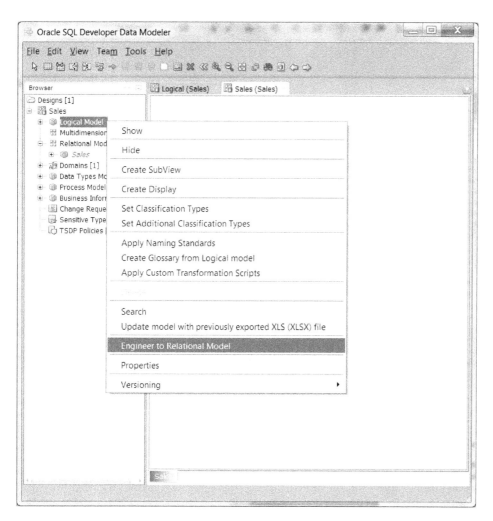

On the **Engineer to Relational Model** window:

- Expand the folders to see the details of the objects.
- Notice that Display object is not in the list.
    - Logical model's Display is not engineer-able to relational.
    - If you need to, 'manually' create any Display specifically on the relational model.
- You select the logical objects (on the left pane) to engineer by checking/unchecking the check boxes.
- When you finish selecting (we are selecting all), click the Engineer button.

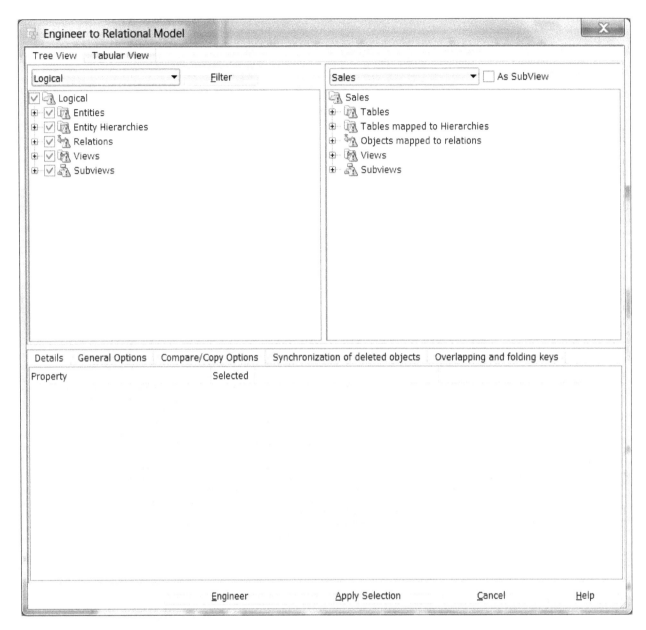

The relational model is now populated with the model objects (tables, views, and so on)

- You can see the objects on both the Browser and diagram. You might need to adjust the diagram to better see the objects.
- On the diagram tables are drawn as boxes (while entities on a logical diagram are drawn as **rounded-corners** boxes)

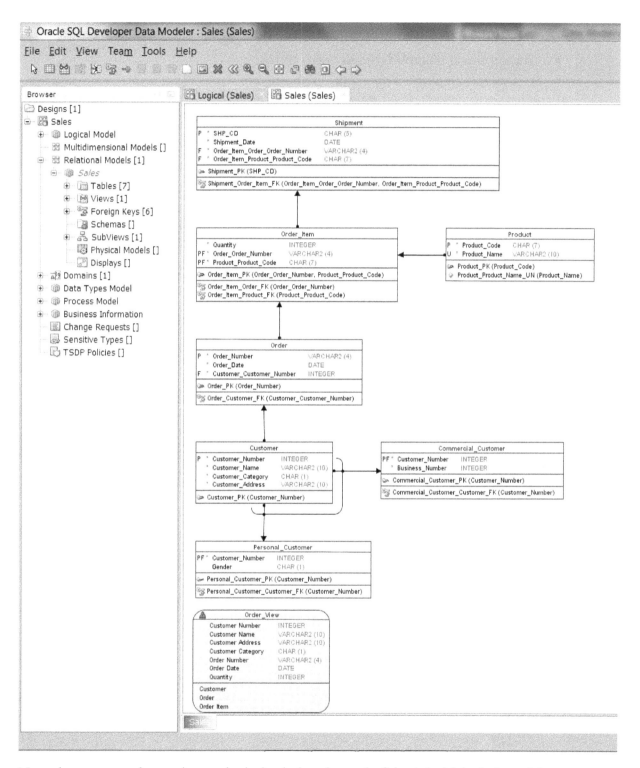

Note that you can also engineer a logical subview, instead of the (whole) logical model.

- You will likely engineer subview by subview if your model is big:
  - Encompassing multiple business areas, and/or
  - You want to implement the model in phases, not the whole at once.
- If you have any subview, it will be seen on the drop-down.

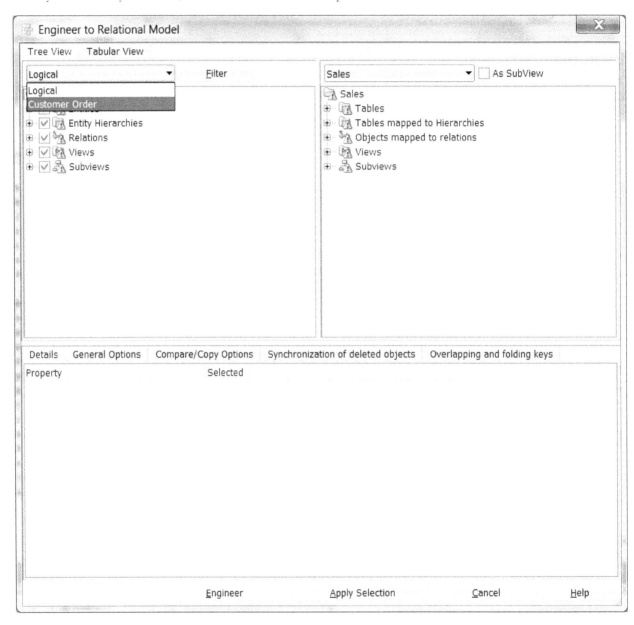

# Direction of Relationship

On the diagram the relationship arrow points from the parent entity (primary key) to the child entity (foreign key), which is my preference.

You can choose the arrow direction by:

- Selecting Tools menu > Preferences.
- On the Preferences window, select Data Modeler > Diagram > Relational Model
- Choose your preferred direction by clicking its radio button.

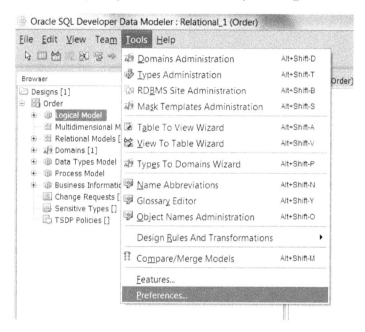

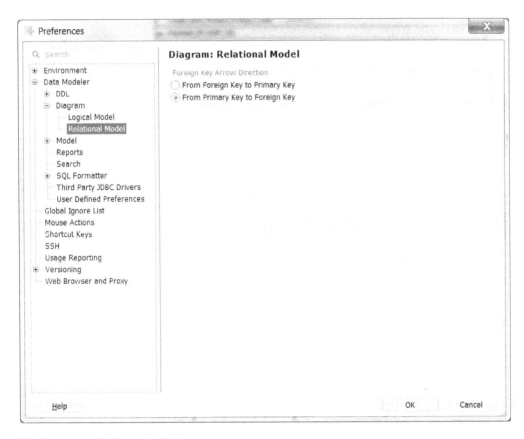

## Relational Model Objects

The relational model has its specific objects, objects that are not available in the logical model or any other implementation technology.

If you expand the Order Item node of both the logical and relational model, you will see that Index object is only available on the relational model. We will create an index on our relational model.

# Creating Index

To add an index, double click on the table, for example Order Item. The Table Properties window will open.

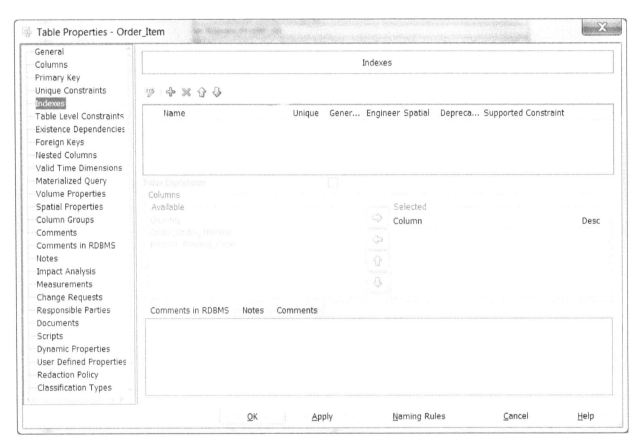

Select Indexes, and click the green +. An index will be added.

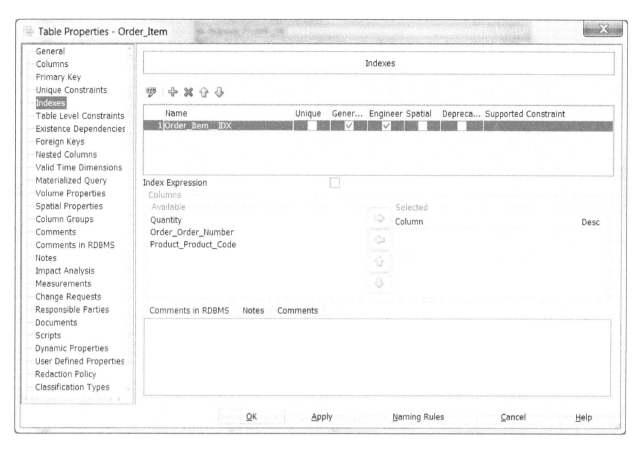

Select the column you want to index, for example, Order Number and Product Code, then click the Add arrow.

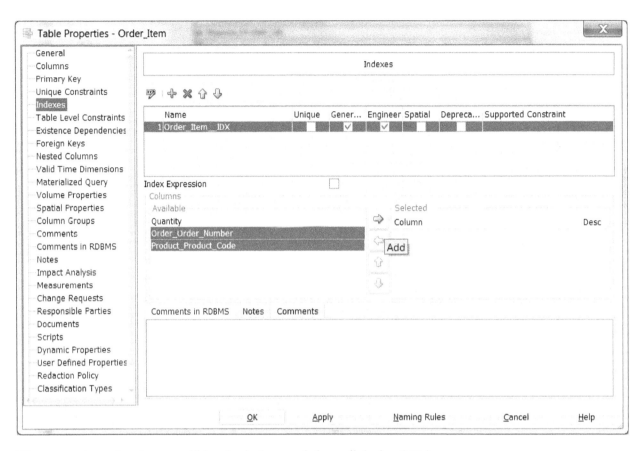

The two selected columns will be the index, and then click the OK button.

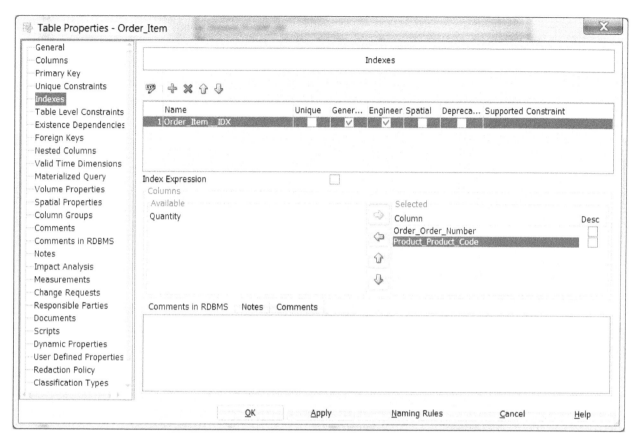

The index is shown on the Browser and the Order Item table on the diagram.

- You might need to resize and adjust the layout to see the index on the diagram.

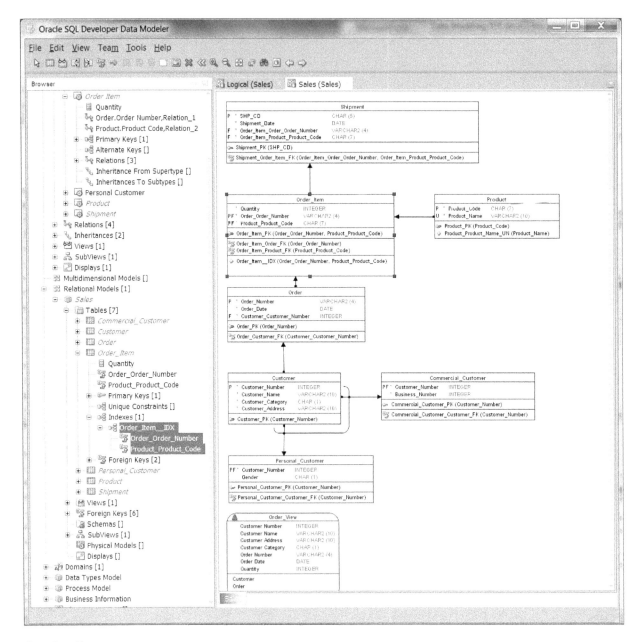

On the diagram:

- The Order_Item_IDX index is shown at the bottom section of the Order Item entity box.
- The index has a diamond tag as shown here.
- You will see later that the index is engineered into the physical model, and ultimately in the generated DDL (Data Definition Language) which we then use to create the Oracle database.

```
                        Order_Item
    *  Quantity                   INTEGER
PF *  Order_Order_Number          VARCHAR2 (4)
PF *  Product_Product_Code        CHAR (7)
─────────────────────────────────────────────────
   Order_Item_PK (Order_Order_Number, Product_Product_Code)
─────────────────────────────────────────────────
   Order_Item_Order_FK (Order_Order_Number)
   Order_Item_Product_FK (Product_Product_Code)
─────────────────────────────────────────────────
   Order_Item__IDX (Order_Order_Number, Product_Product_Code)
```

## Subtype Discriminator

Recall that we have two types of customer:

■ Commercial and Personal

■ We would like to be able to distinguish these two types at the Customer table; hence we have the Customer Category column on the table. To enable this column to serve as such, we need to specify our need on the relational model.

On the relational diagram:

■ Double-click the Customer table to open its Table Properties window.

■ Then, on the Table Properties window, double-click the Customer_Category column to open its Properties window.

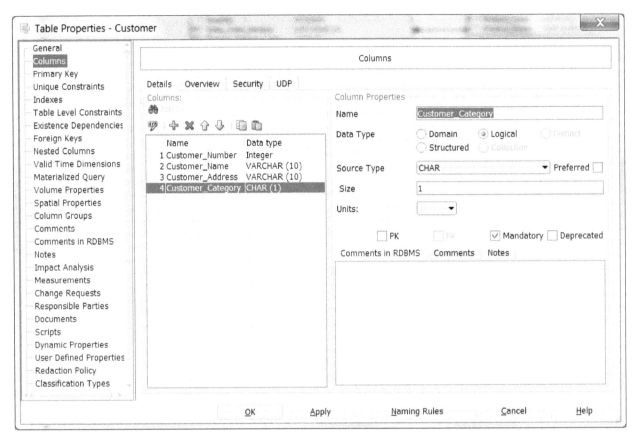

Then, on the Column Properties window, click the Values of "List Of Values".

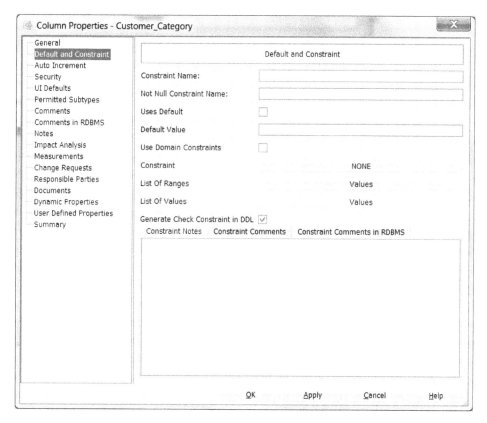

## On the List Of Values window:

- Add two values by clicking the Add button.
- 'C' and 'P', and their descriptions.
- These two values will be the only allowed on the Customer Category column.
- Then, close the window by clicking the OK button.

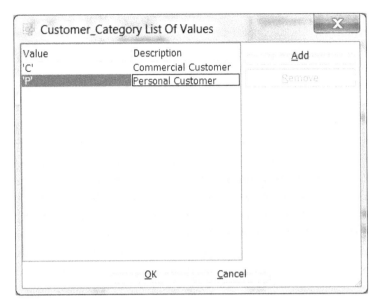

Close the Column Properties and Table Properties window.

Next, we need to ensure the correct population on the two customer subtype tables.

On the relational diagram, double-click the subtype arc.

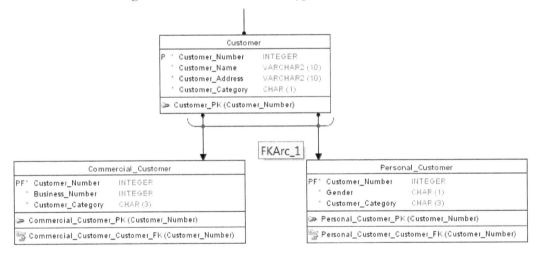

On the General pane of the Arc Properties window:

- Check the Mandatory box.
- Select Customer_Category as the Discriminator Column.
- Then click the Apply button.

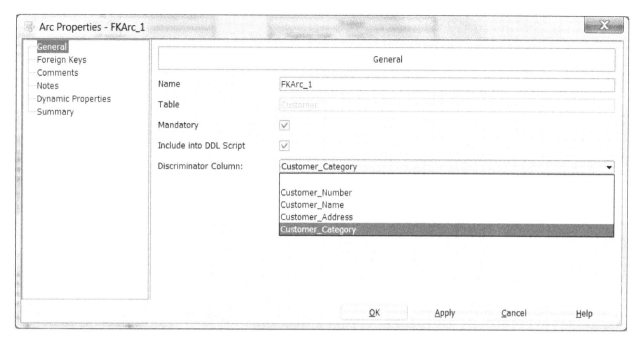

On the Foreign Keys pane, enter the 'C' and 'P' values, then click OK button to close the window.

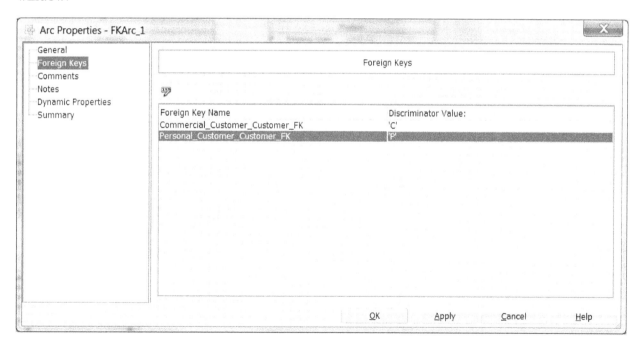

## Constraints and Triggers on the DDL

As a result of the above specifications, when we later generate the DDL script of the relational model, you will see:

- A check constraint on the Customer's Customer_Category column allowing only 'C' or 'P' value.
- A trigger ensuring the Commercial Customer table is the one populated if the Customer's Category column's value is 'C'.
- A trigger ensuring the Personal Customer table is the one populated if the Customer's Category column's value is 'P'.

### Additional Relational Model

You can create more than one relational model from a logical model, which you do so the same as the first one.

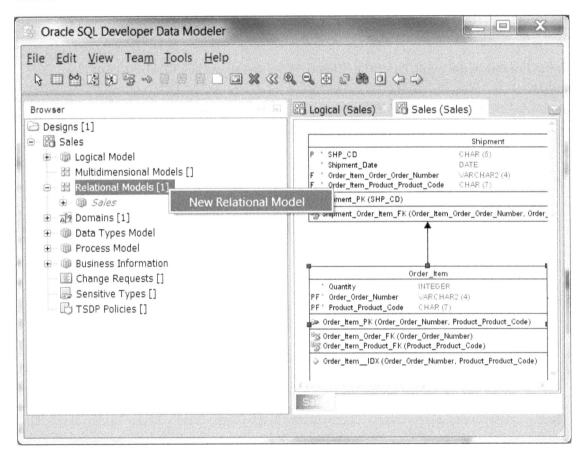

We now have two relational models.

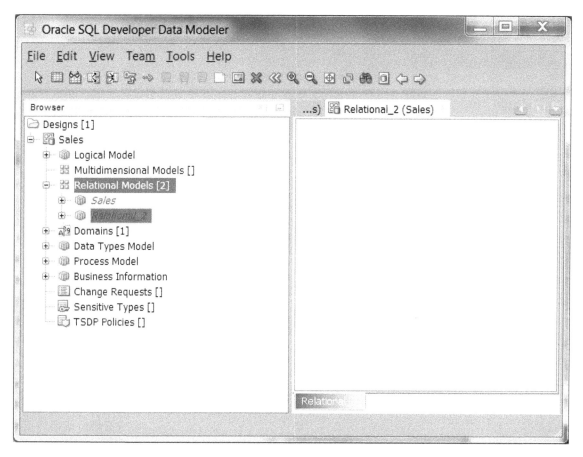

You can then engineer the logical model to the Relational_2.

- Relational_2 can be a different version than the first, i.e. selecting different set of entities and/or attributes (or other model objects, e.g. views).
- We will no longer use the Relational_2 in this book, so delete it.

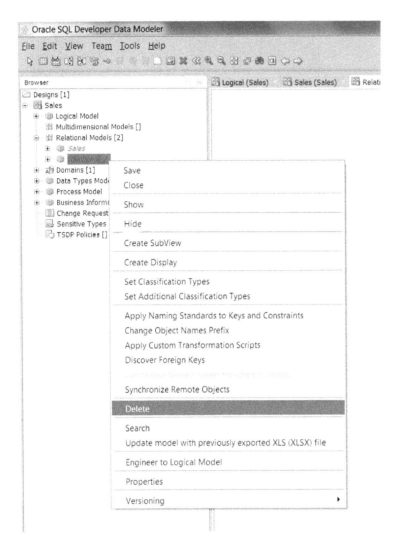

## Abbreviating Names

Relational database product puts a limit on the length of object names.

- Oracle's limit, for example, is 30 characters.
- If you later generate the DDL script and any of the object names (e.g. a table or column name) exceed 30 characters, you will see the error message in the script.

Fortunately Oracle Modeler has a name abbreviating facility.

### Abbreviation CSV

For every name we want to abbreviate, we need to specify it in a CSV file (Comma Separated Value)

- Each record of the CSV file has a format:
  - The name on the right to the comma; its abbreviation on the left.
- I prepared abbrv.csv file (text file) for our use using Windows Notepad.

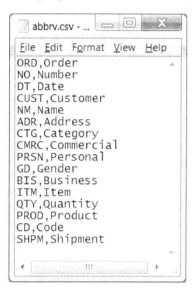

To apply the abbreviations, select Tools then Name Abbreviations.

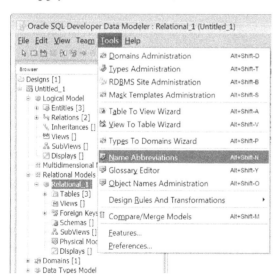

On the "Name Abbreviations" window, we select the csv file, and then click the OK button.

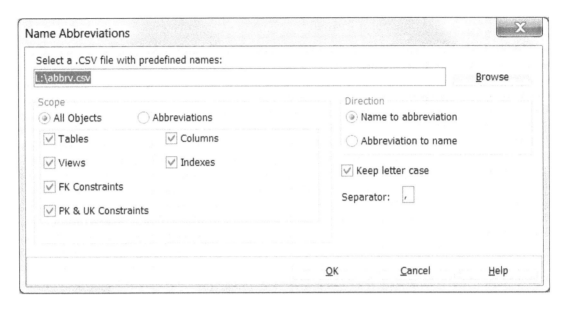

## Abbreviating Log

You will see the log window. You can save if you want to, for your record.

```
View Log                                                                    X

Oracle SQL Developer Data Modeler Names Abbreviations Log.
Date and Time: 2015-11-25 15:22:28 EST
Design Name: Sales

            Standardized Objects:
                    Tables:    7
                    Columns:  17
                    Indexes:   1
                    Views:     1

<<<<< TABLES >>>>>
            Commercial_Customer             -->            CMRC_CUST
            Customer                        -->            CUST
            Order                           -->            ORD
            Order_Item                      -->            ORD_ITM
            Personal_Customer               -->            PRSN_CUST
            Product                         -->            PROD
            Shipment                        -->            SHPM

<<<<< COLUMNS >>>>>
            Business_Number (CMRC_CUST)             -->    BIS_NO
            Customer_Address (CUST)                 -->    CUST_ADR
            Customer_Category (CUST)                -->    CUST_CTG
            Customer_Customer_Number (ORD)          -->    CUST_CUST_NO
            Customer_Name (CUST)                    -->    CUST_NM
            Customer_Number (CMRC_CUST)             -->    CUST_NO
            Gender (PRSN_CUST)                      -->    GD
            Order_Date (ORD)                        -->    ORD_DT
            Order_Item_Order_Order_Number (SHPM)    -->    ORD_ITM_ORD_ORD_NO
            Order_Item_Product_Product_Code (SHPM)  -->    ORD_ITM_PROD_PROD_CD
            Order_Number (ORD)                      -->    ORD_NO
            Order_Order_Number (ORD_ITM)            -->    ORD_ORD_NO
            Product_Code (PROD)                     -->    PROD_CD
            Product_Name (PROD)                     -->    PROD_NM
            Product_Product_Code (ORD_ITM)          -->    PROD_PROD_CD
            Quantity (ORD_ITM)                      -->    QTY
            Shipment_Date (SHPM)                    -->    SHPM_DT

<<<<< INDEXES >>>>>
            Order_Item__IDX (ORD_ITM)               -->    ORD_ITM_IDX

<<<<< PRIMARY KEYS & UNIQUE KEYS >>>>>
            Commercial_Customer_PK (CMRC_CUST)      -->    CMRC_CUST_PK
            Customer_PK (CUST)                      -->    CUST_PK
            Order_Item_PK (ORD_ITM)                 -->    ORD_ITM_PK
            Order_PK (ORD)                          -->    ORD_PK
            Personal_Customer_PK (PRSN_CUST)        -->    PRSN_CUST_PK
            Product_PK (PROD)                       -->    PROD_PK
            Shipment_PK (SHPM)                      -->    SHPM_PK

<<<<< FOREIGN KEYS >>>>>
            Commercial_Customer_Customer_FK (CMRC_CUST) -->    CMRC_CUST_CUST_FK
            Order_Customer_FK (ORD)                 -->    ORD_CUST_FK
            Order_Item_Order_FK (ORD_ITM)           -->    ORD_ITM_ORD_FK
            Order_Item_Product_FK (ORD_ITM)         -->    ORD_ITM_PROD_FK

                            Save        Close
```

You can see now that all the relational names are abbreviated.

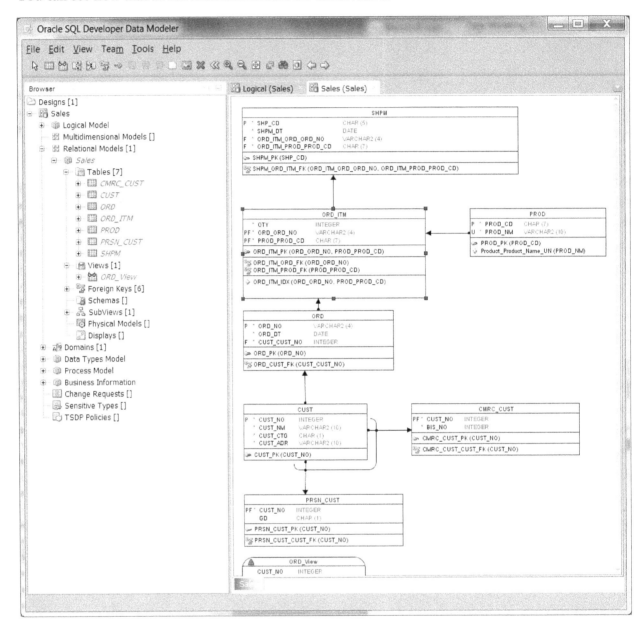

[114]

# Chapter 4: Physical Model

Physical model is for a specific database product, such as the Oracle Database 11g.

## Creating Physical Model

We create a physical model from a relational model by right clicking the relational model

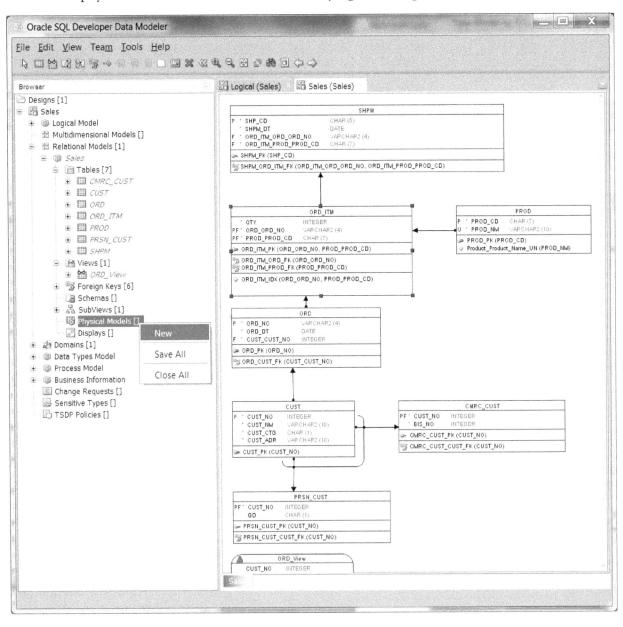

You will be prompted to select the specific database technology for the physical model.

■ Currently, the Oracle Modeler supports the databases as seen on the following "Database Sites" window. Select one as your target physical database and then click the OK button.

■ Physical model does not have its own diagram.

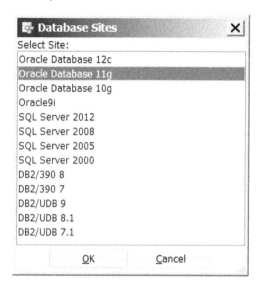

The physical model (named as the database you have chosen) is now populated.

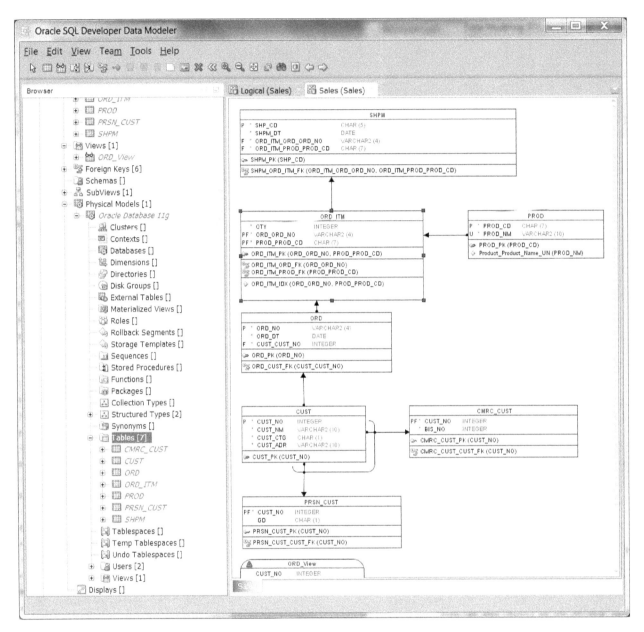

Using the same steps above, you can create more than one physical from a relational model, e.g. in additional to the Oracle Database 11g, you can also create for SQL Server 2012.

## Physical Object

You can add objects on the physical model that are specific to the Oracle database, e.g. Role.

- A role is a set of privileges (permissions) granted.
- When you generate the DDL from the relational model, the role will be available to select

■ And then, when you run the DDL, the role (database object) will be created.

## Creating Role

To create a role:

■ Right click the Roles > New.

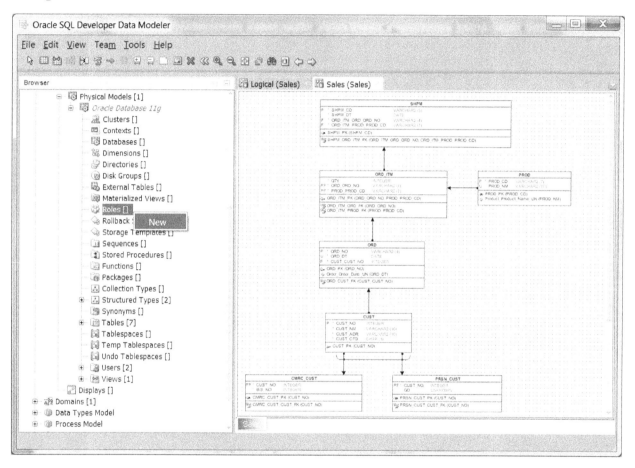

You can specify the role properties, e.g. Name, Identification Type and its Password.

…And its permission by clicking the Permission button and select the tables you want to specify their permission in the role.

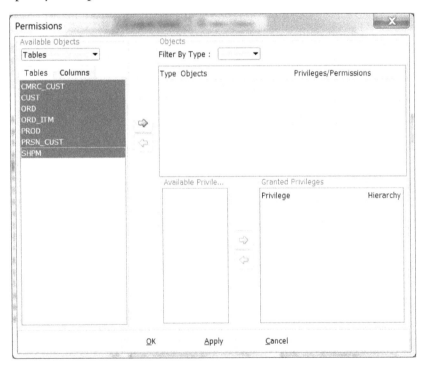

…And the privileges, then click the Apply, and close the window by clicking the OK button.

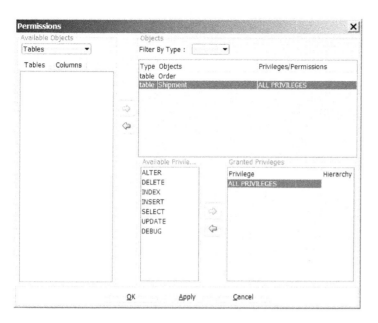

In addition to specifying at table level, you can also:

- Specify at column granularity by selecting a table and then select its column(s) at the Columns tab.
- In addition to table/column, specify on other objects, by clicking the drop-down of the Available Objects.

For example, for the CUST table...

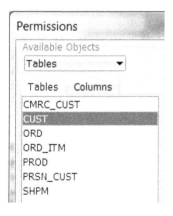

On the Columns tab, you will be able to select the CUST's columns.

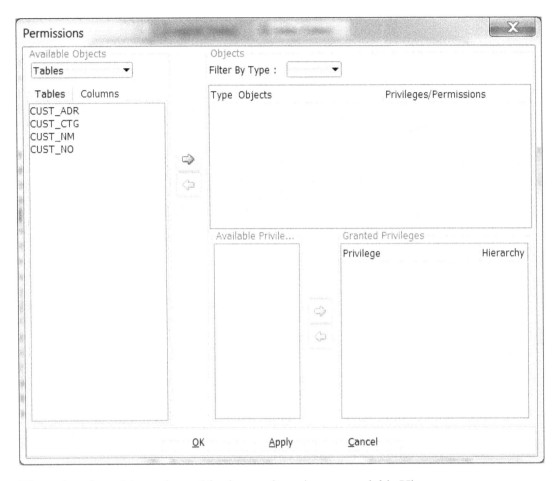

The only other objects than table that we have in our model is View.

So when you select Views, the Order_View will be listed.

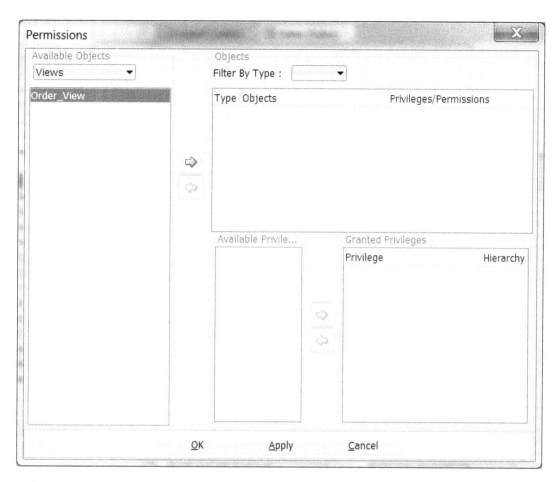

When you are done specifying the role, close the Role Properties window, by clicking the OK button.

You can see the role on the Browser…

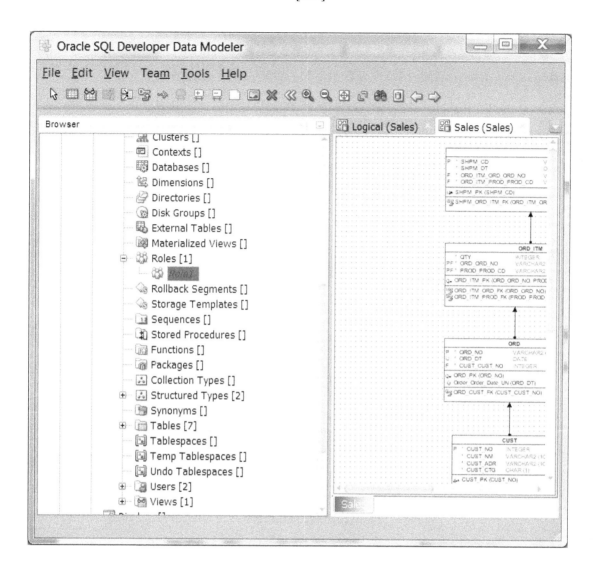

# Chapter 5: Generating DDL (Data Definition Language)

To generate the DDL, select Export, then DDL File from the File menu.

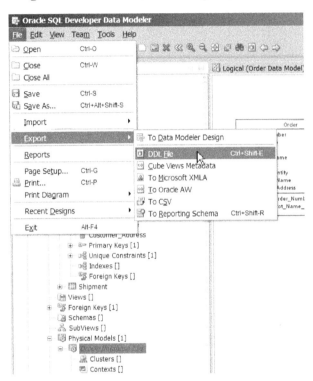

Select the relational model you want to generate its DDL and click the Generate button.

Select only the objects you want to generate their DDL, and then click the OK button.

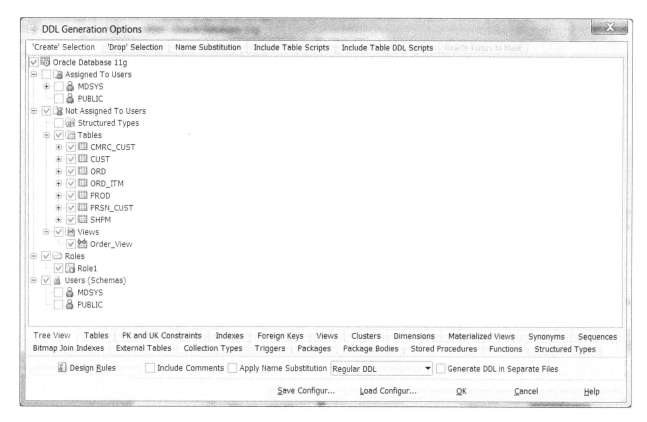

Save the DDL into a file (by clicking the Save button) for later execution to generate the actual tables and other objects (e.g. role) on your database installation.

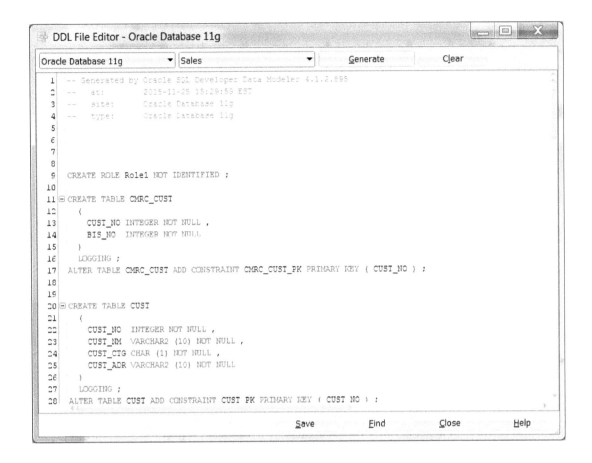

```
 DDL File Editor - Oracle Database 11g                              _  □  X

 Oracle Database 11g      ▼   Sales              ▼      Generate      Clear

  1   -- Generated by Oracle SQL Developer Data Modeler 4.1.2.895
  2   --    at:        2015-11-25 15:29:59 EST
  3   --    site:      Oracle Database 11g
  4   --    type:      Oracle Database 11g
  5
  6
  7
  8
  9   CREATE ROLE Role1 NOT IDENTIFIED ;
 10
 11 ⊟ CREATE TABLE CMRC_CUST
 12    (
 13      CUST_NO INTEGER NOT NULL ,
 14      BIS_NO  INTEGER NOT NULL
 15    )
 16    LOGGING ;
 17   ALTER TABLE CMRC_CUST ADD CONSTRAINT CMRC_CUST_PK PRIMARY KEY ( CUST_NO ) ;
 18
 19
 20 ⊟ CREATE TABLE CUST
 21    (
 22      CUST_NO  INTEGER NOT NULL ,
 23      CUST_NM  VARCHAR2 (10) NOT NULL ,
 24      CUST_CTG CHAR (1) NOT NULL ,
 25      CUST_ADR VARCHAR2 (10) NOT NULL
 26    )
 27    LOGGING ;
 28   ALTER TABLE CUST ADD CONSTRAINT CUST_PK PRIMARY KEY ( CUST_NO ) ;

                             Save      Find      Close      Help
```

# Chapter 6: Generating Database Objects

To generate the database objects we execute the DDL script.

- You can execute the DDL script in SQL Developer.
- If you don't have SQL Developer, you can download it from the Oracle website and use it free of charge. Refer to Appendix for details.

To execute the DDL script in SQL Developer:

- Start your SQL Developer.
- Open the DDL script from where you saved it.

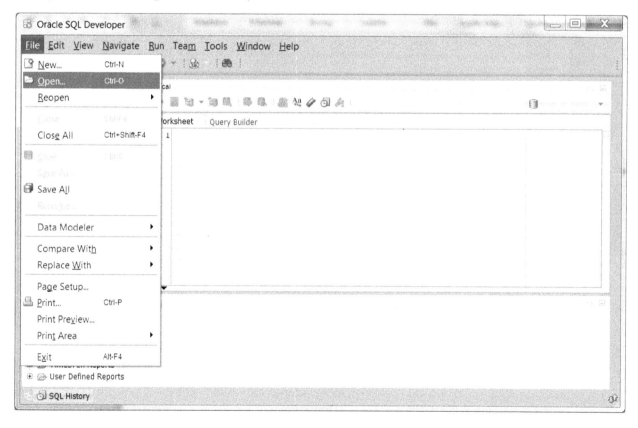

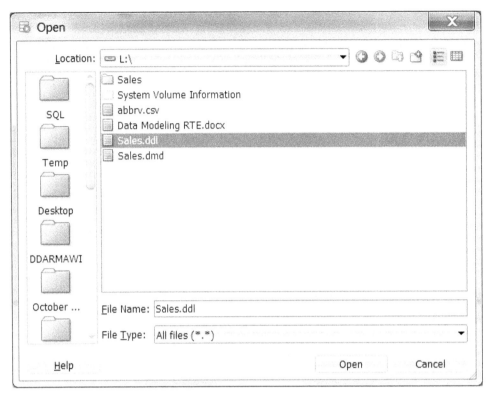

- Run the script.

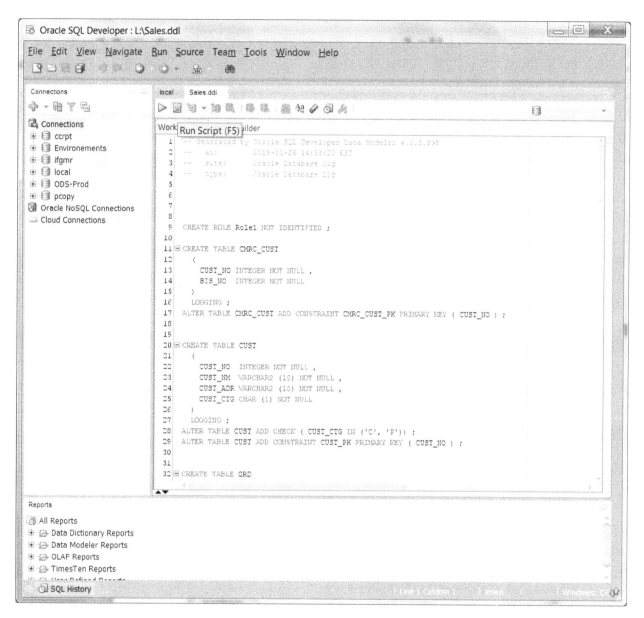

Select the connection to the database where you want to generate the database objects.

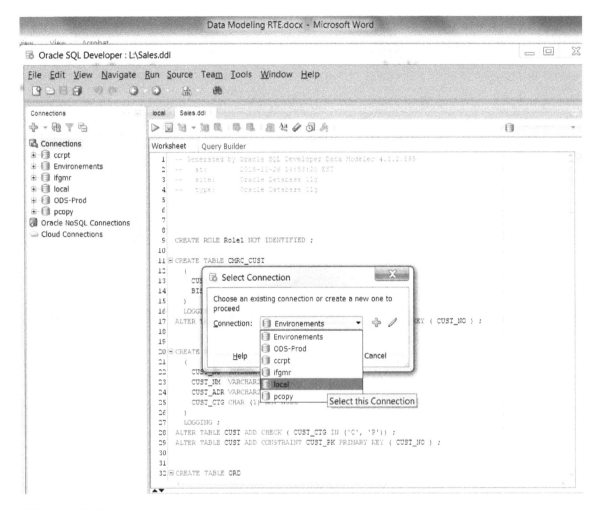

Click the OK button.

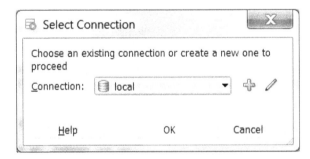

Supply the password when prompted and click the OK button.

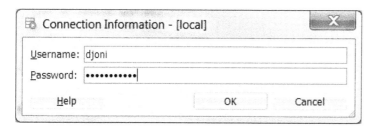

When the execution is successful, you will see the objects created, e.g. the tables and view.

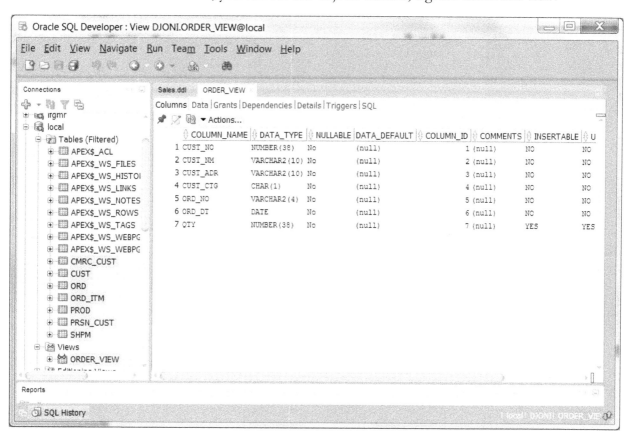

## Part II: Reverse Engineering

In this part we will reverse engineer an existing database back into a logical model.

For some reasons the database that you originally generated from a model might have changed. If the database change is not generated from the model, your model is no longer in synch with the database.

You do reverse engineering to get a model that reflects the current status of a database, to synchronize the model with the database.

- You do a reverse engineering not only for a major change.
- The change can be as small as renaming a table or changing the size of a column.

The reverse engineering consists of the following steps.

- Importing/merging data dictionary into relational model
- Converting abbreviation to name
- Engineer relational to logical model

[135]

# Chapter 7: Importing/Merging Database to Model

For the sake of our example in this book, we will first change the database.

The changes are:
- Add a table called SUPP (Supplier).
- Add a column named SUPP_SUPP_NO and make it a foreign key from the PROD table.

Execute the following script to make the changes.

```
CREATE TABLE SUPP
  (
    SUPP_NO INTEGER NOT NULL,
    SUPP_NM VARCHAR2 (10) NOT NULL
  ) ;
ALTER TABLE SUPP ADD CONSTRAINT SUPP_PK PRIMARY KEY (SUPP_NO);
ALTER TABLE PROD ADD (SUPP_SUPP_NO INTEGER NOT NULL);
ALTER TABLE PROD ADD CONSTRAINT PROD_SUPP_FK FOREIGN KEY (SUPP_SUPP_NO)
REFERENCES SUPP (SUPP_NO);
```

## Importing Data Dictionary

The first thing you need to do to reverse engineer an existing database is to import its data dictionary into a **relational** model in the Data Modeler.

- Make sure you have the model you want to update is opened.

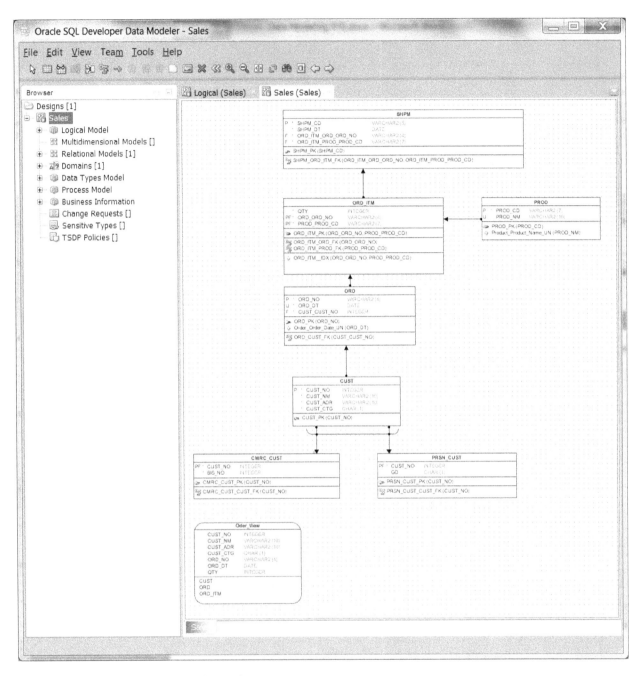

To import a data dictionary, follow these steps:

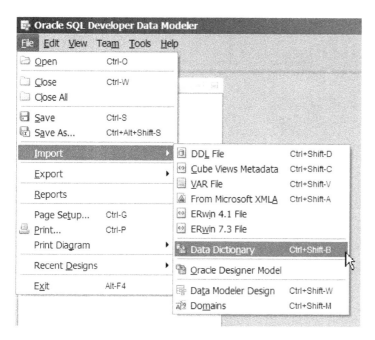

The Data Dictionary Import Wizard will show up.

- As you can see on the left pane, the import process has four steps to follow.
- The first step is to connect to the database you want to import its data dictionary.
- You can add a connecting by clicking the Add button.

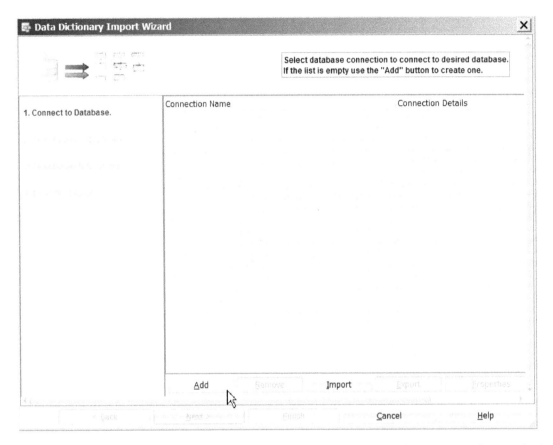

On New/Select Database Connection window enter a Connection Name of your choice, an authorized Username (user id) and its Password, also the Hostname, Port number, and the database's SID. To make sure the connection info you entered is good, click the Test button.

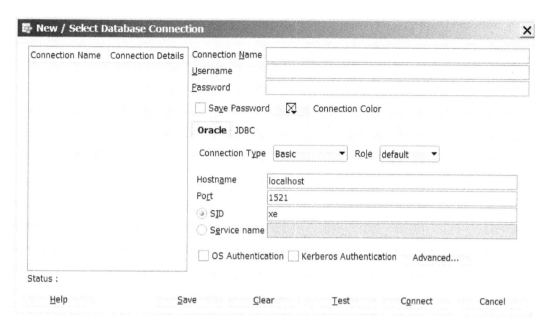

If the connection is good, you will see Success on the Status (bottom left corner) of the window; then click the Connect button.

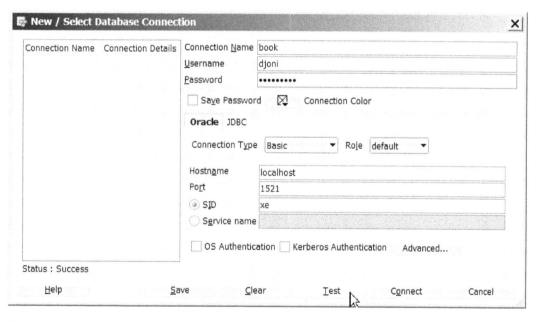

Back on the Data Dictionary Import Wizard, select the book connection you've just created, then click the Next button.

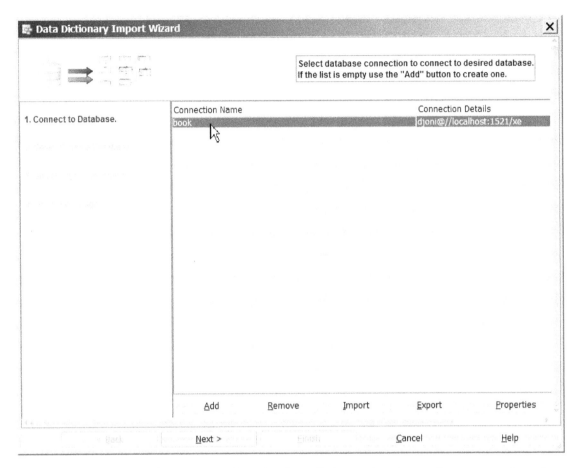

On the Select Schema/Database, select the data dictionary's schema (in my case the schema name is DJONI), then click the Next button.

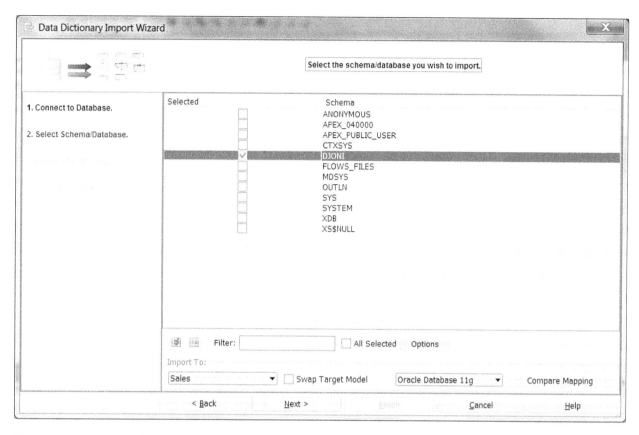

You can select the tables you want to import individually by clicking its selection box on the left of the object.

- You may need to import changes only, which you will then use to update the existing data model.

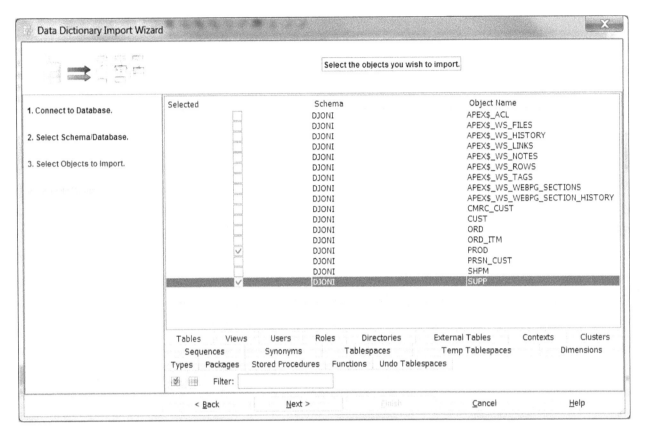

Next, click the Views tab to select the views to import.

- If we know for sure that there's been no change on any view, we might not want to import any; and similarly to the other model objects, e.g. role in our example.

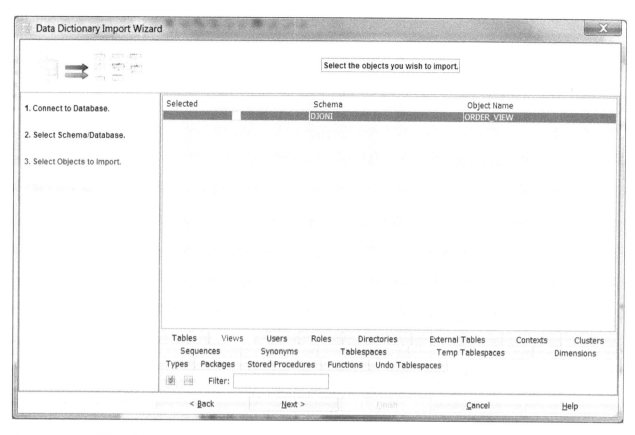

A summary of the objects to be imported is shown; click the Finish button.

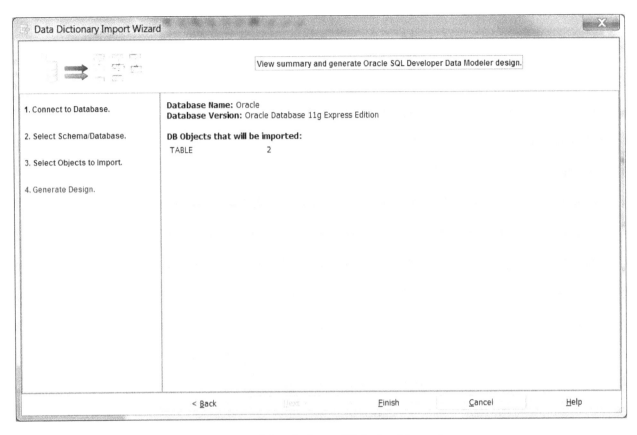

You will be presented the Compare Models window. Click the Merge button.

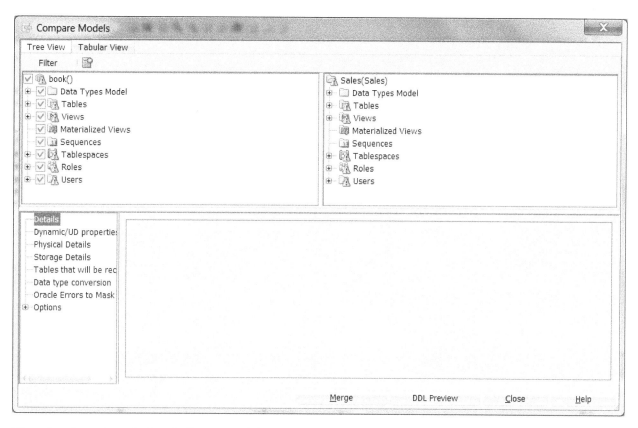

The visual on the relational diagram might get unclear. Adjust the size.

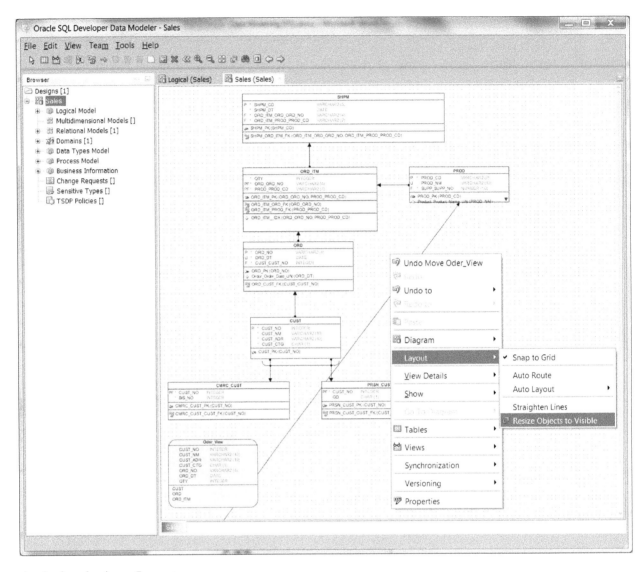

And, also do Auto Layout.

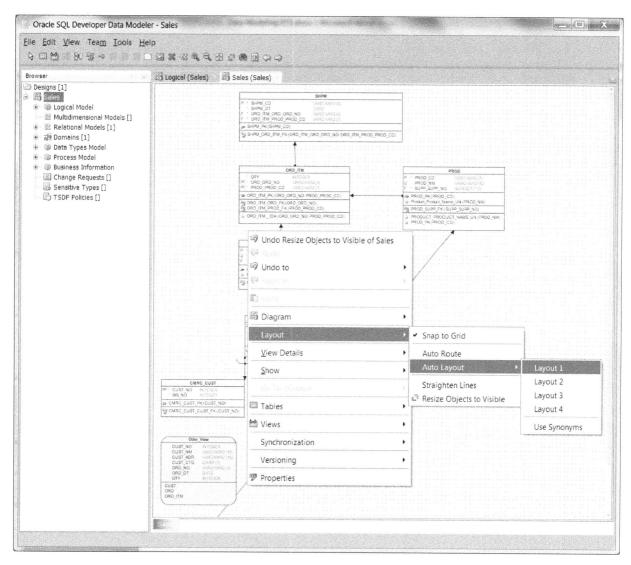

You should now be able to see the changes: the new SUPP table and the new SUPP_SUPP_NO column on the PROD table.

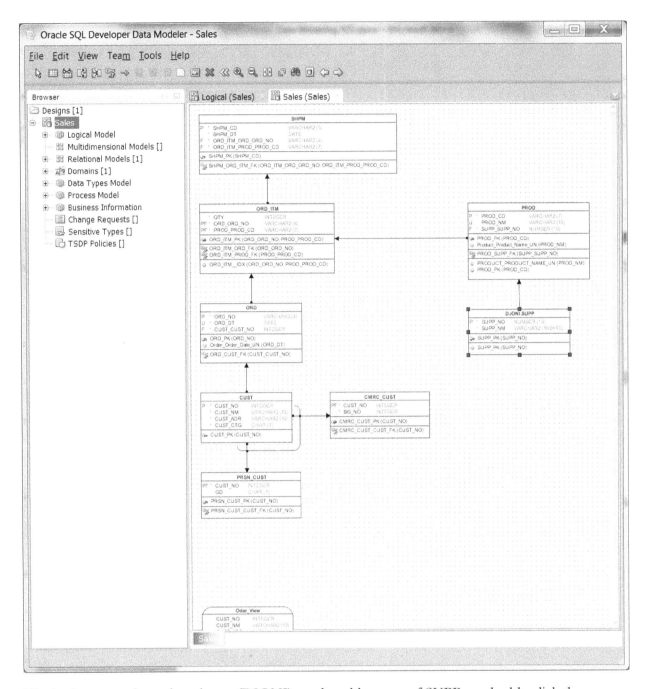

We don't want to have the schema (DJONI) on the table name of SUPP, so double-click the table to open the Table Properties window.

- Select a blank (instead of DJONI) from the Schema drop-down list.
- Click Apply and then click OK to close the window

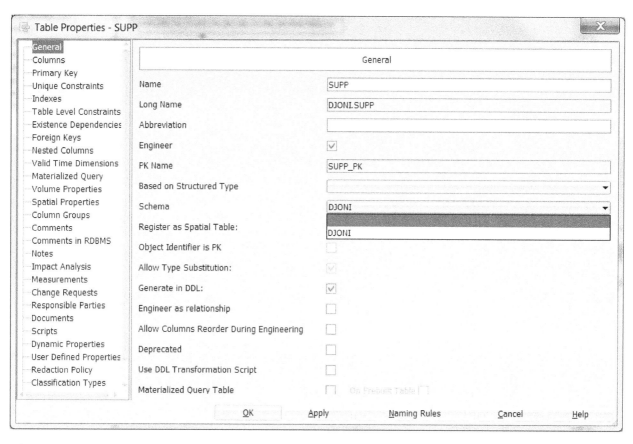

The table name is now just SUPP.

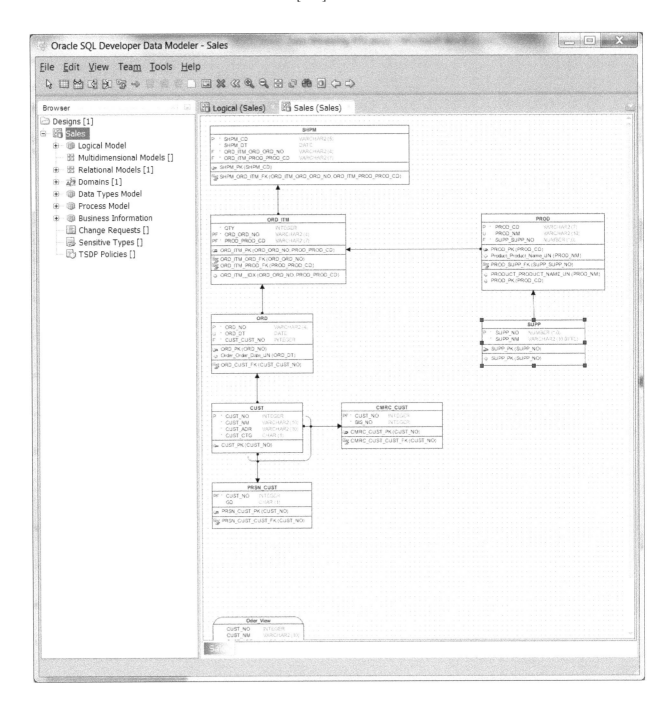

## Chapter 8: Converting Abbreviation to Name

In the relational model we imported the names of tables and their columns abbreviated. In the logical model we would like the names, not abbreviation.

To rename the abbreviations back to the names, open the Name Abbreviations from the Tools menu.

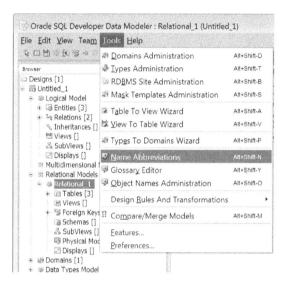

Select the abbreviation csv file.

- Make sure the csv file has all the new abbreviations introduced in the database; in our case it is the SUPP

And then:

- On the Direction, select the "Abbreviation to name" option
- To have the full names in their original case (i.e. mixed case), un-check the "Keep letter case" box
- Click the OK button to start the renaming

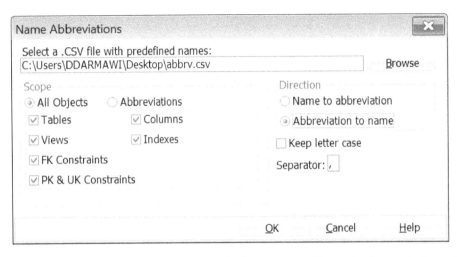

When the un-abbreviation process is done, you will see its Log window. Close it.

```
View Log                                                                          X

Oracle SQL Developer Data Modeler Names Abbreviations Log.
Date and Time: 2015-11-27 13:38:04 EST
Design Name: Sales

         Standardized Objects:
                Tables:   8
                Columns:  21
                Indexes:  3
                Views:    0

<<<<< TABLES >>>>>
          CMRC_CUST                        -->              Commercial_Customer
          CUST                             -->              Customer
          ORD                              -->              Order
          ORD_ITM                          -->              Order_Item
          PROD                             -->              Product
          PRSN_CUST                        -->              Personal_Customer
          SHPM                             -->              Shipment
          SUPP                             -->              Supplier

<<<<< COLUMNS >>>>>
          BIS_NO (Commercial_Customer)     -->              Business_Number
          CUST_ADR (Customer)              -->              Customer_Address
          CUST_CTG (Customer)              -->              Customer_Category
          CUST_CUST_NO (Order)             -->              Customer_Customer_Number
          CUST_NM (Customer)               -->              Customer_Name
          CUST_NO (Personal_Customer)      -->              Customer_Number
          GD (Personal_Customer)           -->              Gender
          ORD_DT (Order)                   -->              Order_Date
          ORD_ITM_ORD_ORD_NO (Shipment)    -->              Order_Item_Order_Order_Number
          ORD_ITM_PROD_PROD_CD (Shipment)  -->              Order_Item_Product_Product_Code
          ORD_NO (Order)                   -->              Order_Number
          ORD_ORD_NO (Order_Item)          -->              Order_Order_Number
          PROD_CD (Product)                -->              Product_Code
          PROD_NM (Product)                -->              Product_Name
          PROD_PROD_CD (Order_Item)        -->              Product_Product_Code
          QTY (Order_Item)                 -->              Quantity
          SHPM_CD (Shipment)               -->              Shipment_Code
          SHPM_DT (Shipment)               -->              Shipment_Date
          SUPP_NM (Supplier)               -->              Supplier_Name
          SUPP_NO (Supplier)               -->              Supplier_Number
          SUPP_SUPP_NO (Product)           -->              Supplier_Supplier_Number

<<<<< INDEXES >>>>>
          ORD_ITM__IDX (Order_Item)        -->              Order_Item_IDX
          PROD_PK (Product)                -->              Product_PK
          SUPP_PK (Supplier)               -->              Supplier_PK

<<<<< PRIMARY KEYS & UNIQUE KEYS >>>>>
          CMRC_CUST_PK (Commercial_Customer) -->            Commercial_Customer_PK
          CUST_PK (Customer)               -->              Customer_PK
          ORD_ITM_PK (Order_Item)          -->              Order_Item_PK
          ORD_PK (Order)                   -->              Order_PK

                            Save        Close
```

You will see the full names (with their mixed cases).

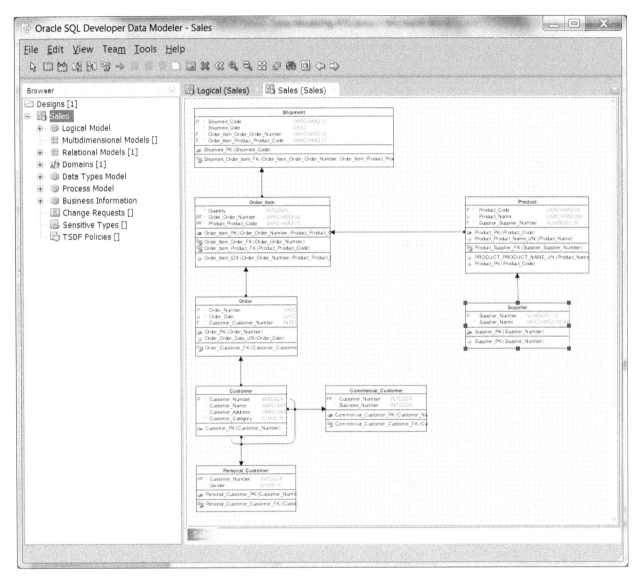

We are now ready to create the logical model from the relational model.

# Chapter 9: Engineer into Logical Model

To engineer the relational model to a logical model, right-click the book (note that book is the name of the connection we use to import the data dictionary) and select "Engineer to Logical Model".

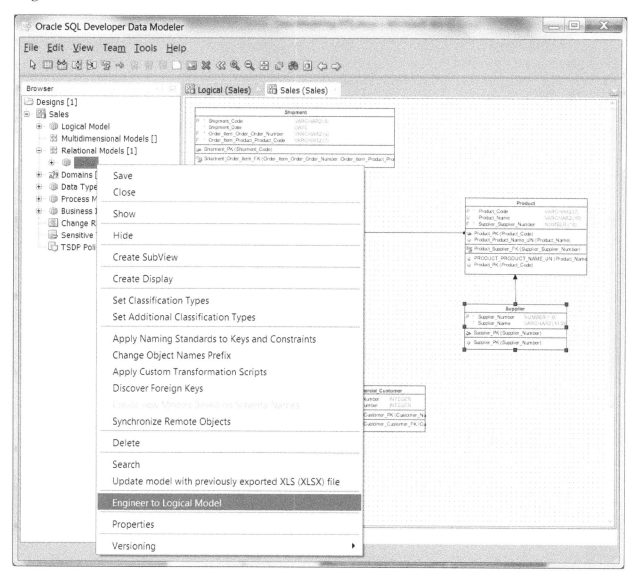

On the Engineer to Logical Model window click the Engineer button.

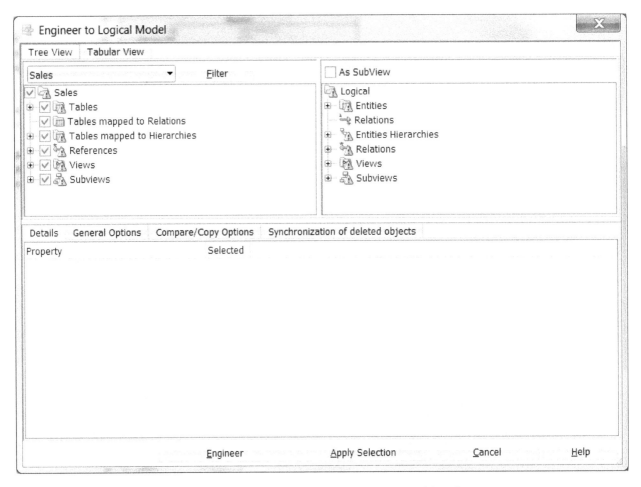

You should now see the resulting logical model on the Browser and its diagram.

- Adjust the diagram for you convenient visual the way you did earlier on the relational diagram.

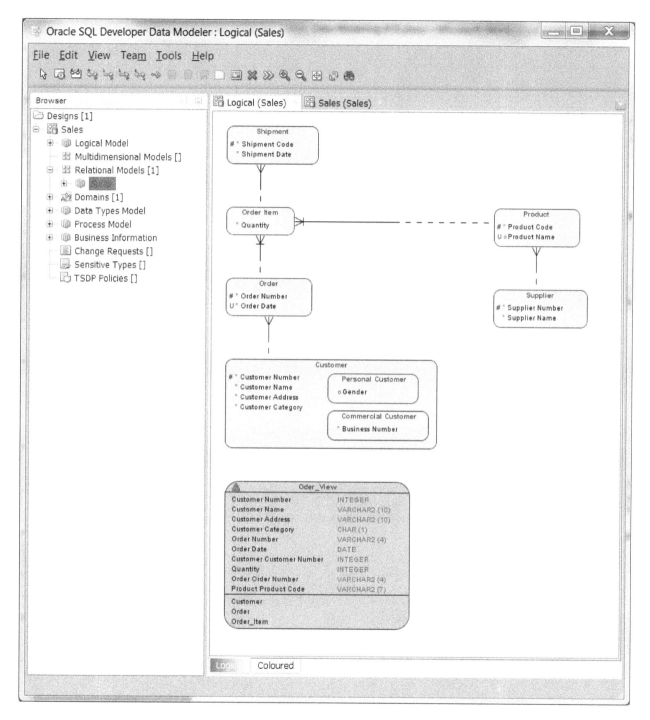

## Saving the Revised Model

The Sales model has been updated, if you want to preserve the earlier model, we can save the updated into a different design.

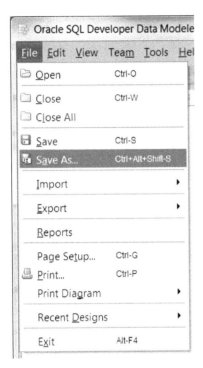

For example:

[160]

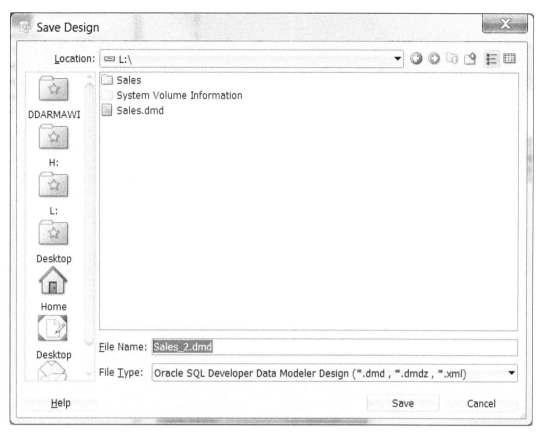

The design is now Sales_2.

# Appendix A: Installing the Tools

## SQL Developer Data Modeler

The Data Modeler's formal name is SQL Developer Data Modeler. It is a free of charge software from Oracle.

At the time of writing this book, the Oracle web page from which you can download the SQL Developer Data Modeler is http://www.oracle.com/technetwork/developer-tools/datamodeler/downloads/index.html

Click the Accept License Agreement and select to download one that is suitable for your platform.

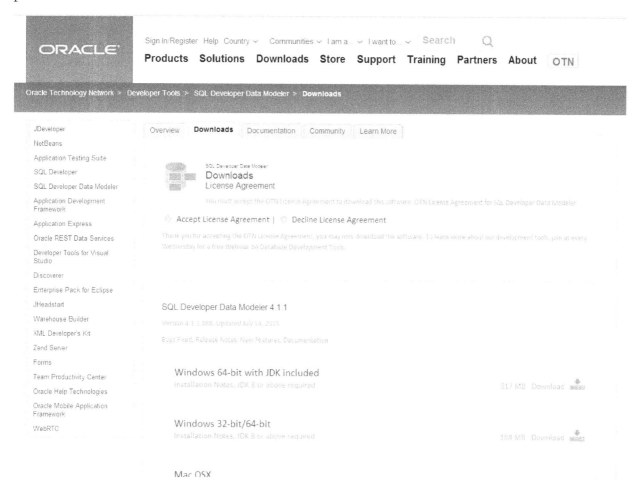

No installation is actually needed; you just need to extract the downloaded zip file into a directory of your choice.

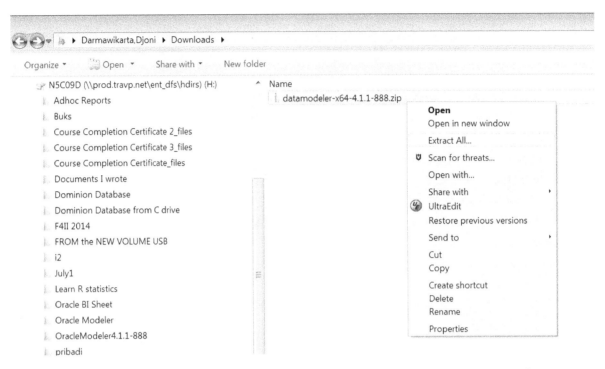

Find the datamodeler.exe on the datamodeler subfolder, and double-click it to start the Data Modeler. Note: You may want to create a shortcut on your Desktop, so you don't need to go the subfolder to start the Data Modeler.

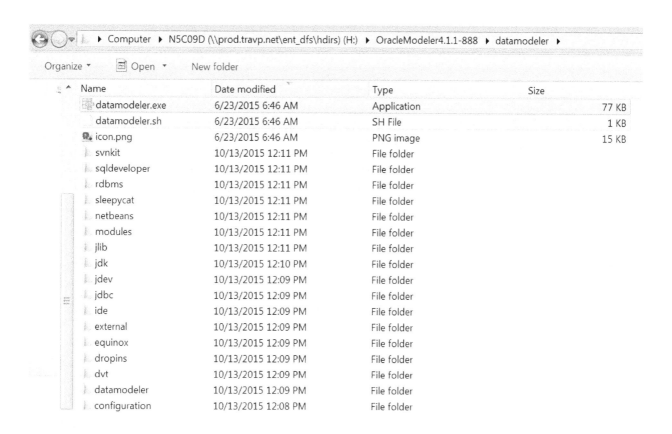

The Start Page tab will be shown. If you don't want to see the page the next time you start the Data Modeler, de-select the "Show on Startup" checkbox.

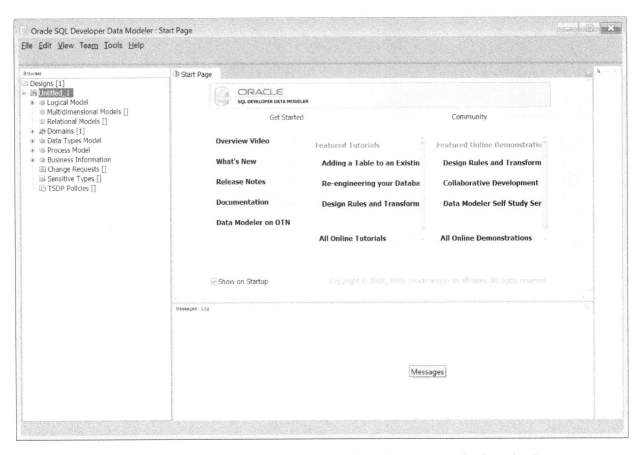

If you want to specifically see the Start Page tab, go to the Help menu and select the Start Page.

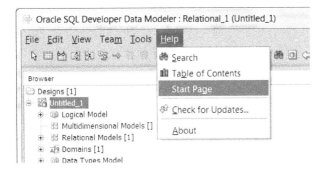

The Start Page tab will be opened.

[166]

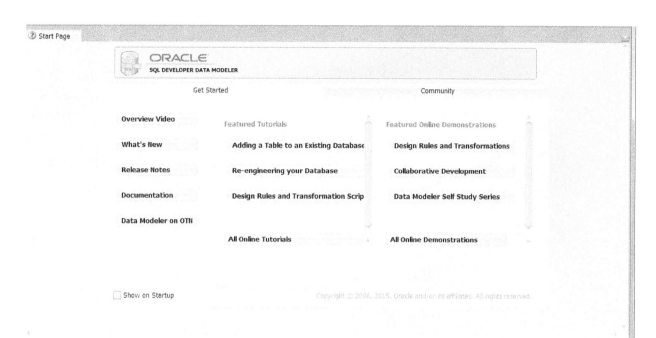

## Database Express Edition

Go to http://www.oracle.com/technetwork/indexes/downloads/index.html

Locate and download the Windows version of the Oracle Database Express Edition (XE). You will be requested to accept the license agreement. If you don't have one, create an account; it's free.

Unzip the downloaded file to a folder in your local drive, and then, double-click the setup.exe file.

You will see the Welcome window.

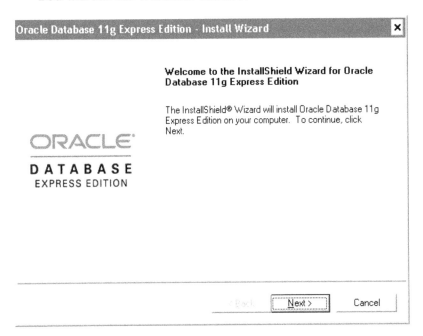

Click the Next> button, accept the agreement on the License Agreement window, and then click the Next> button again.

The next window is the "Choose Destination Location" window.

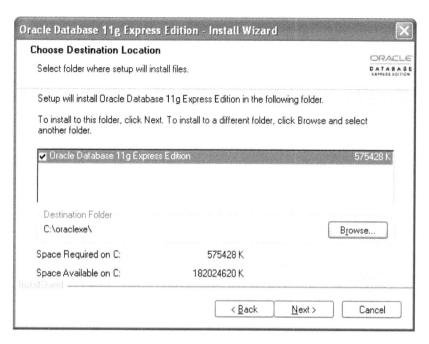

Accept the destination folder shown, or click the Browse button to choose a different folder for your installation, and then click the Next> button.

On the prompt for port numbers, accept the defaults, and then click the Next> button.

On the Passwords window, enter a password of your choice and confirm it, and then click the Next> button. The SYS and SYSTEM accounts created during this installation are for the database operation and administration, respectively. Note the password; you will use the SYSTEM account and its password for creating your own account, which you use for trying the examples.

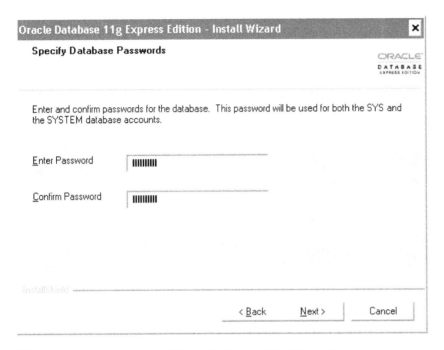

The Summary window will be displayed. Click Install.

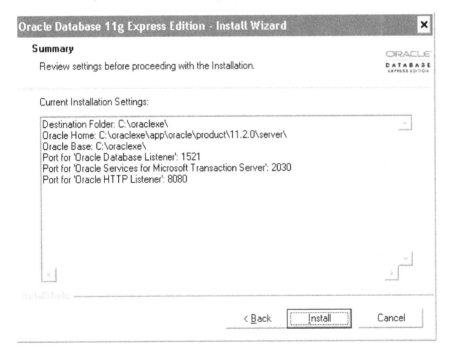

Finally, when the Installation Completion window appears, click the Finish button.

Your Oracle Database XE is now installed.

## SQL Developer

SQL Developer is optional to try the book examples. Instead of using SQL Developer, you can run DDL on SQL*Plus for example. But I recommend using the GUI of the SQL Developer.

Go to http://www.oracle.com/technetwork/indexes/downloads/index.html

Locate and download the SQL Developer. You will be requested to accept the license agreement. If you don't have one, create an account; it's free.

Unzip the downloaded file to a folder of your preference. Note the folder name and its location; you will need to know them to start your SQL Developer.

When the unzipping is completed, look for the sqldeveloper.exe file.

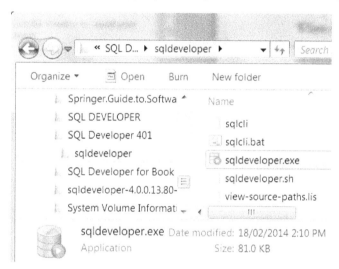

You start SQL Developer by opening (double-clicking) this file.

You might want to create a short-cut on your Desktop.

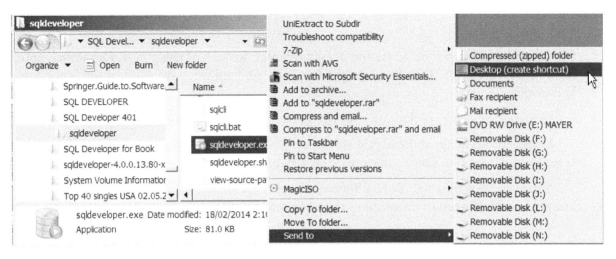

You can then start your SQL Developer by double-clicking the short-cut.

Your initial screen should look like the following. If you don't want to see the Start Page tab the next time you start SQL Developer, un-check the *Show on Startup* box at the bottom left side of the screen.

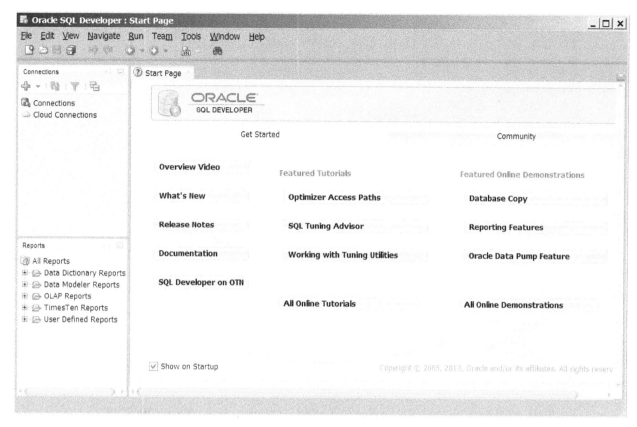

For now, close the Start Page tab by clicking its x.

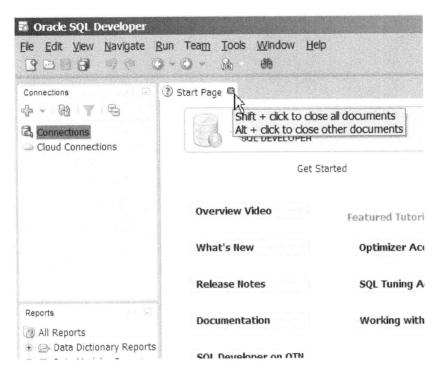

## Creating Connection

To work with a database from SQL Developer, you need to have a connection.

A connection is specific to an account. As we will use the SYSTEM account to create your own account, you first have to create a connection for the SYSTEM account.

To create a connection, right-click the Connection folder.

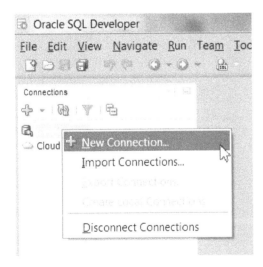

On the New/Select Database Connection window, enter a Connection Name and Username as shown. The Password is the password of SYSTEM account you entered during the Oracle database installation. Check the Save Password box.

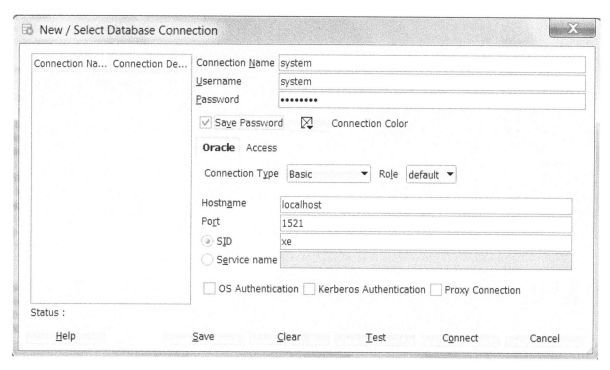

When you click the Connect button, the *system* connection you have just created should be available on the Connection Navigator.

A Worksheet is opened for the system connection. The Worksheet is where you type in source codes.

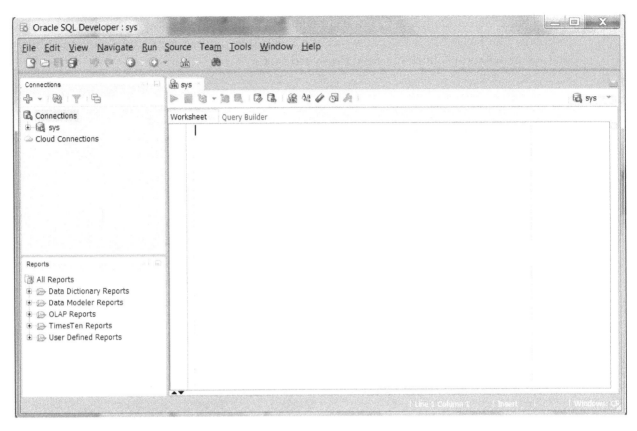

## Creating Database Account

You will use your own database account (user) to try the book examples.

To create a new account, expand the system connection and locate the Other Users folder at the bottom of the folder tree.

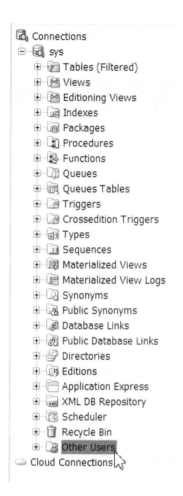

Right click and select Create User.

Enter a User Name of your choice, a password and its confirmation, and then click the Apply button. You should get a successful pop-up window; close it.

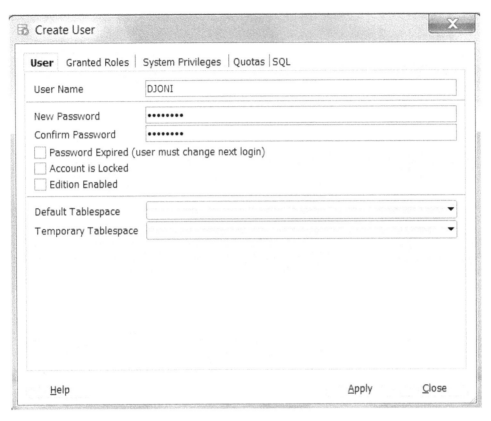

On the Granted Roles tab, click Grant All, Admin All and Default All buttons; then click the Apply button. Close the successful window and the Edit User as well.

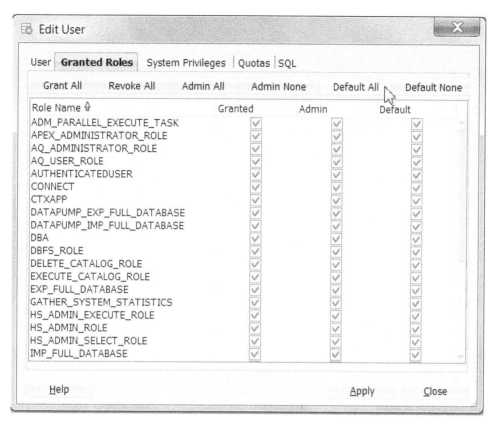

## Creating Your Connection

Similar to when you created system connection earlier, now create a connection for your account.

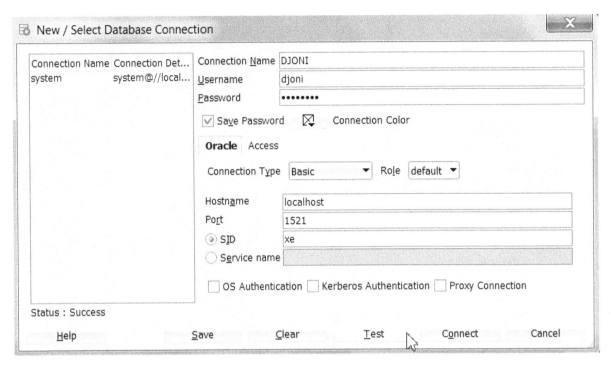

Click the Connect button. A worksheet for your connection is opened (which is *DJONI* in my case).

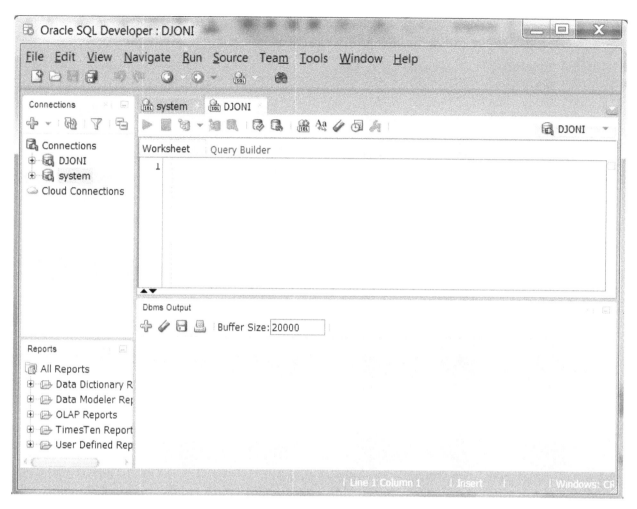

## Deleting the *system* Connection

Delete the *system* connection, making sure you don't use this account mistakenly. Click Yes when you are prompted to confirm the deletion. Your SQL Developer is now set.

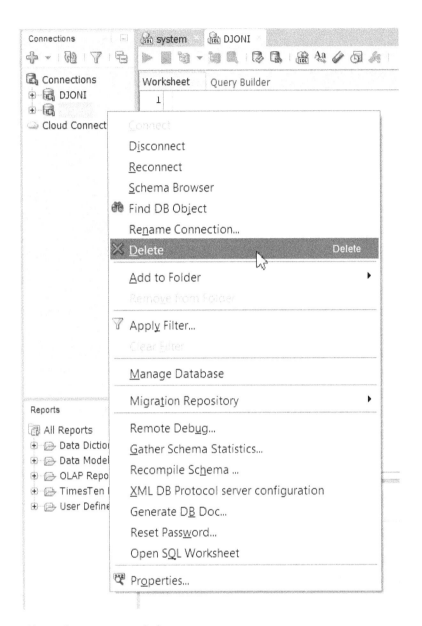

Close the *system* worksheet.

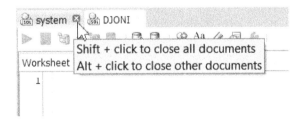

# Appendix B: Diagramming

You will often use the ER diagram, particularly that of the logical model, to communicate with the business users. As such you want to make sure the objects in the diagram are presented clearly.

This chapter shows you how to use the features of the Oracle Modeler useful for improving the diagrams.

## Showing Grid

The Grid helps to visually see the locations of objects on the ER diagram, for example their positions relative to one another.

To show the grid, right-click on the empty space; select "Show" then "Grid".

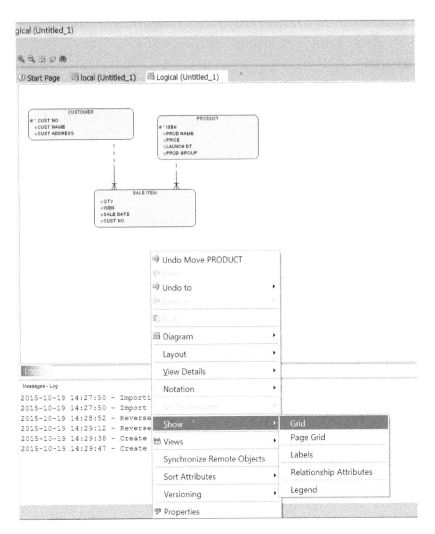

Grids (dots) will be visible on the diagram canvas.

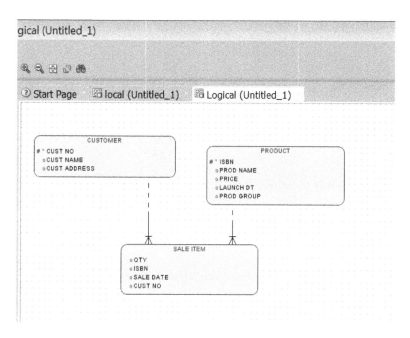

## Moving Objects

You can move objects such as an entity by selecting/holding and moving it; for example, below I moved the Customer entity to the right. Note that the relationship line also moves.

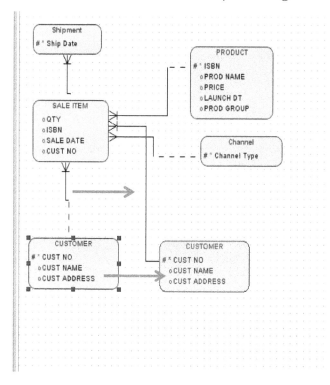

The position of Customer entity will now looks like.

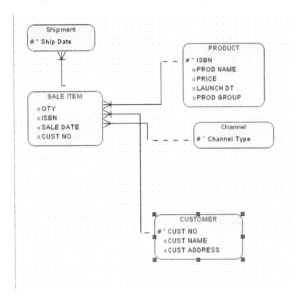

Note that you can also move a relationship line without moving its entities. Make sure you disable the Auto Route.

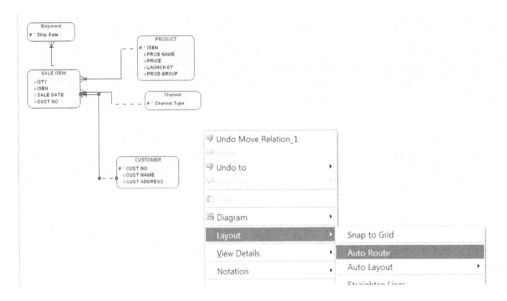

## Snapping to Grid

So when you move an entity or add a new one, the entity will automatically be snapped (aligned) to the grid.

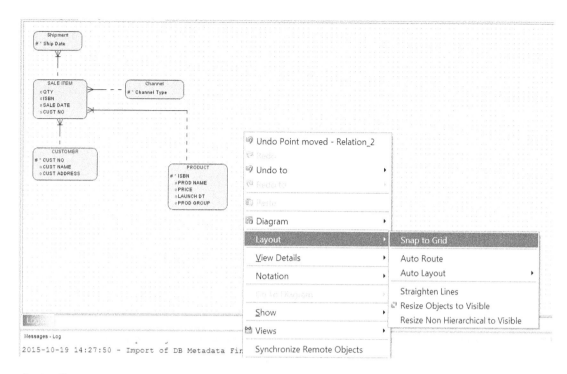

## Auto Layout

The auto layout, which you access by right-clicking on the empty space; select the "Layout", then "Auto Layout", and select any one of the four Layout's.

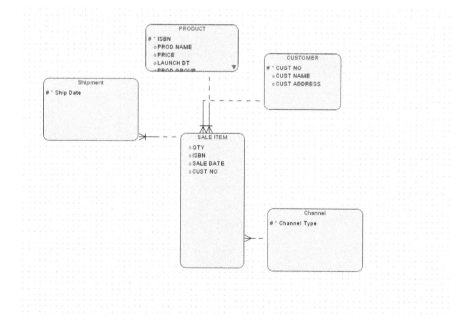

The entities will be re-arranged. Relationship crowfeet's will move to point upward and leftward. This arrangement is a desirable convention.

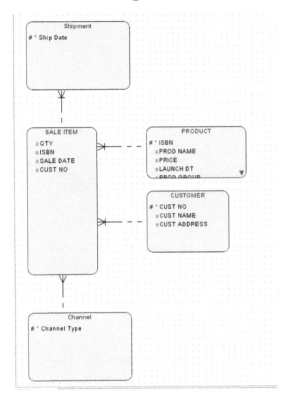

## Resize to Visible

The down arrow at the bottom right-hand corner indicates there's more; such as that on the PRODUCT entity.

To show completely, right click on a blank space. Select Layout then the "Resize Objects to Visible".

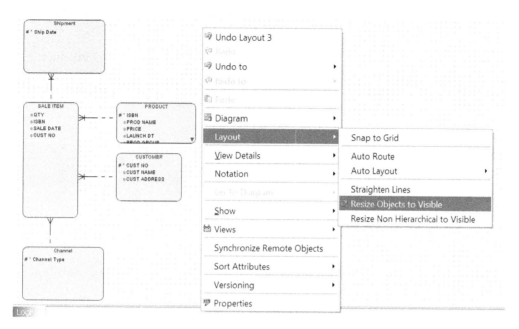

All attributes of the Product entity is now shown, and there's no more down-arrow on the entity.

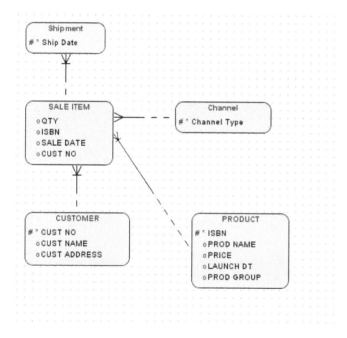

## Bending Relationship Line

You might not like the direction of the relationship line connecting Sale Item to Product. To …, you need to first add an elbow by right-clicking the line at the point where you want to add an elbow, and then select "Add Elbow".

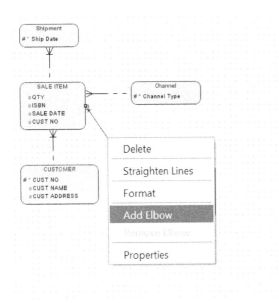

Then, shape the line by moving the elbow point to your desired position.

Note that you can have more than one elbow.

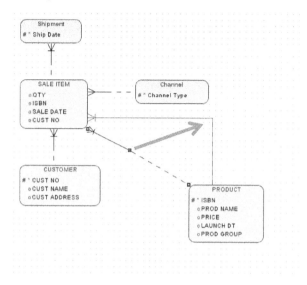

## Aligning Top/Left

Select the entity you want to be the reference (anchor) entity for the alignment, and then select the other entities to be aligned to the reference entity, and then select "Align Left" or "Align Top" from the "Edit" menu.

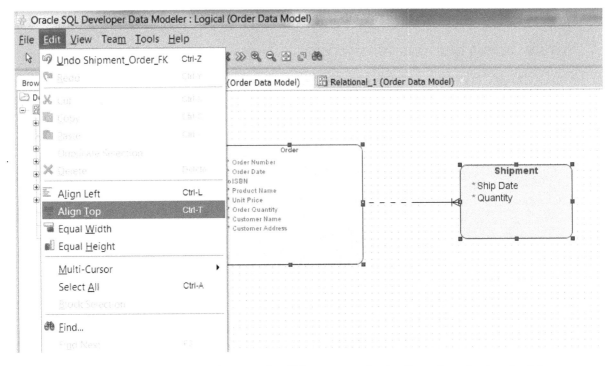

Here I selected the Order entity first, so the Shipment entity is aligned to the 'top' of the Order entity.

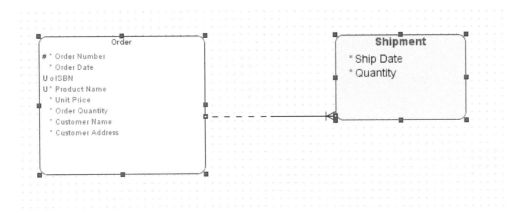

## Equal Width/Height

In a similar manner, you can adjust the size of the entities, making them to the same width or height.

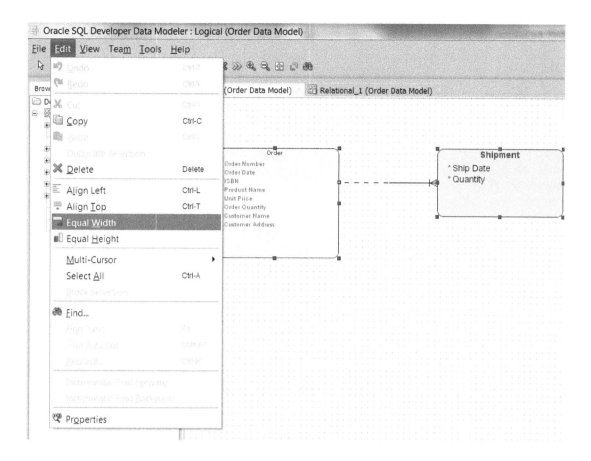

# Index

www.ingramcontent.com/pod-product-compliance
Lightning Source LLC
Chambersburg PA
CBHW080411060326
40689CB00019B/4211